PERCEPTION OF OTHER PEOPLE

FRANZ FROM

Perception of Other People

TRANSLATED BY
ERIK KVAN AND
BRENDAN MAHER

Columbia University Press
NEW YORK AND LONDON
1971

Franz From

is Professor of Psychology at Copenhagen University.

Copyright © 1971 Columbia University Press
ISBN: 0-231-03402-4
Library of Congress Catalog Card Number: 76-138295
Printed in the United States of America

IN MEMORY OF
EDGAR RUBIN

Translator's Preface

THE LANGUAGE OF PHENOMENOLOGY is inevitably subtle and complex. In no language is it easy to develop a vocabulary that will communicate a description of experience to somebody else while retaining a convincing congruence with the primary qualities of the experience itself. This problem is doubly difficult when the task is to translate such a vocabulary from one language to another, and triply so when the prevailing psychological models of the one language-culture are different from those of the other.

To Erik Kvan belongs the credit for the major achievement of rendering Professor From's Danish manuscript into English. The present writer has contributed a retranslation of various parts of the text where the basic translation seemed in need of elaboration or where the idioms of the English language and Anglo-American psychology were not fully caught by a literal translation of the Danish. To Professor Kvan should go the credit for this labor, and to the present writer such criticisms as might arise from infelicities in the final version.

A key concept in this work relates to the term "experience." In colloquial English it is customary to distinguish between an *experience* of an inner emotion and a *perception* of an external event. Thus one "experiences" a sense of frustration but "perceives" an obstacle to the attainment of one's goals. From a phenomenological point of view this distinction might be regarded as irrelevant, inasmuch as both the perception and the experience refer to inner states of consciousness and might well be classified together. When faced with a threat, for example, we might perceive the threat and experience fear. But this separation of a visual input from a visceral input is artificial: in consciousness the separation is not evident and the total state might justly require only a single term. From has preferred to use a single term, best translated as *experience*. Although the sense of the unity of this process would be most obviously served by using one English word, the well-established distinction between perception and experience in English usage has been retained in the belief that communication will be better as a result.

At times, the same word has been translated into the English "observe," where the emphasis in the context is directed toward the external event and its characteristics rather than the phenomenology of the observer. With this exception, however, the translation has been developed with a terminology that accentuates the concern with conscious phenomena and de-emphasizes objective description of events.

For the American reader it might be helpful to discuss here not only technical matters of translation but, more significantly, the place of this kind of work in systematic psychology generally. As the method employed is, in essence, introspective, it would be deceptively simple to assume that the purpose of the approach is to arrive at systematic descriptions of consciousness—a goal of demonstrated sterility at the time of the rise of behaviorism. Such is not the case. It is necessary, instead, to approach From's work with an awareness of the role played by Gestalt psychology in the study of perception and the place of phenomenal reports in the methodology of Gestalt investigations. The positive contribution of perceptual processes to the provision of *Prägnanz* has been, of course, a key observation in Gestalt psychology. At the heart of such demonstrations lies the technique of presenting the subject with a stimulus of either no planned meaning or only partially completed as a meaningful object and recording the reports of the subject as he perceives it. Closure and other resulting phenomena of perceptual distortion or addition are so well established that they appear in the literature of perception almost in the guise of axioms.

At the Psychological Laboratory of the University of Copenhagen, under the initial leadership of Edgar Rubin, these processes have been studied as they might be discerned in interpersonal perception. Rubin was at pains to point out that the concept of closure is functionally related to the concept of redundancy: if we can see a complete circle when the stimulus circle is in fact only partially complete, then the addition of the missing part to the stimulus is unnecessary. Rubin applied this consideration to the study of redundancy in language in a little-known paper * published in Danish antedating and anticipating many of the concepts of contemporary theory. Rubin's own investigations were focused upon the perception of the speech of others, and he was able to show in operation the same processes that were already well established in the investigation of visual form perception. He suggested, further, that the tendency of perceptual systems to construct complete percepts on the basis of incomplete stimuli should be understood in evolutionary terms: this tendency is functional and enables the perceiver to operate effectively most of the time in the face of "insufficient" stimulus input or under conditions of impaired observation. A perceptual system that responded only and precisely to the exact characteristic of stimulus input would be both dangerous and unreliable. In the case of the perceptual constancies the proposition was self-evident, but in the case of interpersonal perception it had not been previously developed.

Contemporary work in the area of interpersonal perception in the United States and Britain has been dominated, in one form or another, by an interest in the role of motive states in determining percepts. Underlying much of this work has been the influence of concepts of projection and repression with their concomitant implication of erroneous or maladaptive processes interfering with the "normal" operation of the perceptual mechanism. From considers the effect of motive states, but in the context of a position from which perceptual extrapolations and additions are assumed to be both inevitable and normal. He attempts, in other words, to shift

* *Om Forstaaelighedsreserven og om Overbestemthed.* In. Til Minde om Edgar Rubin, Nordisk Psykologis Monografiserie No. 8, Copenhagen, 1956.

the emphasis from the individual motivational characteristics of the perceiver to the question of *general* processes operating in the perception of other persons analogous to those operating in the perception of impersonal stimuli. This shift in emphasis is both old and new. It is old in the sense that it restores to the study of this problem a set of concepts and techniques that have long been used in demonstrations of simple visual perceptions. It is new in the sense that it points to a set of questions that have largely been ignored by modern students of individual differences in the perception of other people.

From's approach is not experimental in the accepted sense of the word. He works, as most Gestalt psychologists have, with demonstrations rather than experiments. His task is that of description and analysis rather than manipulation and measurement. It is obviously only a beginning, but a beginning that may lead to considerable future development.

BRENDAN MAHER

Foreword

BY

HENRY A. MURRAY

For too long have too many of us English and American psychologists been deprived of intellectual news from the Laboratorium at Copenhagen. Thwarted by our linguistic deficit, most of us have gained no more than bits and pieces of information regarding, for example, the phenomenological experiments that have been undertaken there since the reign of Edgar Rubin.

But now there is no longer any raison d'être for such an outcast state of ignorance. Professor Kvan has broken the semantic barrier and here before us is a volume that describes in plain English the most far-reaching (I would guess) of the Danish extensions of phenomenology—an extraordinary expedition which was initiated and carried on for several years by Professor From's cognitive processes in conjunction with a series of varied and ingenious empirical researches.

This unique treatise will no doubt be ostracized at first sight by those confirmed apostles of John B. Watson from whose realm of discourse everything "mentalistic" is excluded. But even in the adaptable majority of psychologists the digestion of this book will very probably be punctuated now and again by spasms of perplexed surprise, so different from their accustomed diet are some of its ingredients. The worthiest of these readers, however, should soon be welcoming each recurrence of perplexity as the starting point of fresh reflections on unsettled basic issues, reflections which are very likely to result in a propitious expansion of their field of scientific vision as well as in enough new ideas for further researchers to keep flocks of experimenters busy for years to come.

In the advancement of Gestalt psychology—to the emergence of which Rubin's ambiguous figure-ground demonstrations contributed appreciably—the data that were generally sought, the data from which principles were derived, consisted of precise qualitative descriptions of immediate extrospective experiences, mostly of visual experiences of inanimate, stationary (though sometimes moving) presentations. Adherence to this so-called phenomenological method—marked by theory-free descriptions of the appearance of things without analysis into predefined elements or concepts—was declared (by Köhler for example) to be the proper way for psychologists to begin anew and to proceed for some time to come. Explanatory theories would be arrived at in due course. And so it proved. By this method much knowledge was amassed about the products of the sense-organizing and categorizing perceptual processes in the head of the observer (e.g., the figure of the "dipper" in the sky); but no new knowledge was either sought or gained, of course, about the nature of the observed entities as such (e.g., the physicochemical properties of the stars which are seen in that shape).

In the present work, Professor From, a former student of Rubin, has conformed to the phenomenological tradition by collecting descriptions of immediate experiences of external entities. But he has extended his predecessors' scope of concern by selecting, for the most part, as targets of observation behaving human beings, engaged, say, in overt spatial locomotions and object manipulations; and by this choice he has provided opportunities for each observer to experience (as we all do) immediate impressions either of momentary psychic states or processes (e.g., intentions, hesitations, alterations of intention, evaluations, feelings), or of presumptively more enduring personological properties, within the head of the behaving person.

Here then, in striking contrast to traditional experiments in the sphere of perception, the object at the focus of the observer's attention (in most cases a human being acting within a naturalistic setting) possesses properties the investigation of which is the appointed task of a psychologist. And so, on being told that this is the case, that Professor From's typical set-up is that of one or more persons witnessing the situational transactions of one or more other persons (the actors), one might suppose (in these days of the so-called—alas!—behavioral sciences) that the aim in view was to gain more knowledge, either (1) about the overt reactions of the actors under varying conditions, or (2) about the style or ability of the witnesses as observers and interpreters of the behavior of the actors. All surmises of this sort, however, are canceled at the very outset.

The author tells us, first of all, that to understand his problem "it is of the greatest importance to distinguish between two things: on the one hand, we have the person as he appears in our experience . . . his experienced behavior, his experienced characteristics—on the other hand . . . his—in some scientific sense—'factually existing' behavior and characteristics." And then we are informed—and this may surprise some readers—that the author's plan was to devote himself solely to the study of the first of these two distinguishable things, not at all to the study of the second thing. The adoption of this single orientation would necessarily exclude the possibility (1) of comparing the first thing (the witness's experience of what occurred or existed) with the second thing (what "actually" occurred or existed, insofar as this could be approximately determined), and therefore (2) of estimating the degree of validity of the first thing—where it should be placed on a continuum reaching from a sheer hallucination or delusion at one pole to a veridical observation or intuition at the other. As it happened, this single orientation was maintained whenever it came to the experiencing of another person's psychic state or purpose: the other person was never asked, for instance, to describe his state or purpose as *he himself* experienced it. But when attention was focused on an observer's description of the overt actions of another person (as exhibited, for example, in a moving picture), the single orientation was not constantly adhered to: in several experiments the author (presumably after repeated examinations of the film) is able to tell us exactly what the observed person actually did do from moment to moment. Having obtained this record of what "factually" occurred, the author was in a position to identify (and sometimes to explain in a revealing way) a number of significant common errors in the observers' reports (reconstructed memories) of the actors' behavior sequences. Let this suffice as a preliminary delineation of Professor From's major areas of concern.

Besides habituating himself to the mainly phenomenological orientation of this treatise, the reader must become intimately acquainted with a set of rather uncommon, though suitable, terms which the author introduces and defines as he proceeds with his lucid expositions of various classes of relevant events. Starting with the (above-mentioned) simplest of these classes of events, Professor From says that the behavior of another person is given in our experience as an "undifferentiated totality" with two synchronous yet analytically distinguishable aspects: (1) *a material aspect,* consisting, for example, of the person's facial expressions, body postures, muscular movements, and situational effects; and (2) *a mental aspect,* consisting, say, of an emotion, evaluation, or intention, which is assumptively occurring within the person's head, this mental aspect being given *"in and with"* the material aspect.

Notable here is the use of one valuable verb, "experience," to embrace the operation of two traditionally differentiated, overlapping, processional subsystems. Where Professor From speaks of *experiencing* from moment to moment (1) the material aspect *and* (2) the mental aspect of the activity of a person "out there" in the environment, other psychologists might choose to speak of (1) *perceiving* (i.e., observing) from moment to moment the (overt, visible, objective) physique and physical transactions of that person *and* of (2) concurrently *intuiting* (i.e., spontaneously and synchronously apprehending, inferring, or apperceiving) his successive (covert, invisible, subjective) states of mind—his feelings, thoughts, or purposes—or, in other words (say, through empathic imagination), of having involuntarily and almost instantaneously arrived at (i.e., been presented with) a possible interpretation, explanation, or prediction of that person's perceptible behavior. It is not necessary to say any more here about this largely semantic issue, because the author's preferred concepts are clearly defined and consistently employed and none of us should have much difficulty in following the course of his expositions.

To better equip the reader for what is coming, however, the meaning of four new or not-often-encountered words—*sens, stamp, action potential,* and *psychoid*—should be briefly indicated at this point. The new word *sens* was invented by the author to serve as a generic term for a number of somewhat different orienting psychic factors (such as want, aim, intention, plan, meaning), any one of which may be experienced now and again as governing the ongoing action sequence of another person.

Very often the psychic aspect of an observed span of activity is saliently experienced by us not so much as a transient *sens* related to the particular situation that momentarily confronts the actor but rather as a more or less enduring personological disposition, trait, or ability which (we unconsciously presume) has been manifested in the past and will be manifested in the future for some time to come. A simple or compound characteristic of this sort is called a *stamp.*

After we have had a series of such experiences of another individual's personality, we begin to conceive of him as the possessor or composite of numerous *action potentials*—things he can and will do—and hence things we keep expecting him to do under releasing conditions. In other words, we commonly become *set* to experience another manifestation of this or that *stamp* or *action potential* in an old friend, and if he or she acts in a markedly different way we are likely to be (unpleasantly or, less often, pleasantly) surprised, in which case we may not experience with confidence any definite *sens* (psychic aspect) to account for the unusual behavior.

Also unfamiliar to the majority of English and American psychologists is the useful word *psychoid,* which in this treatise refers to anything visible or audible that evokes in us a simultaneous experience of the occurrence of a *sens* (e.g., purpose) or of the existence of a *stamp* (e.g., trait) in another person. The simplest example of a *psychoid* has already been given, namely, the material aspect of the overt motor activity of another person when, and only when, this is experienced by us in conjunction with some mental entity. In everyday life, speech—expressive and/or directional—constitutes the largest class of significant *psychoids.* Here the material aspect consists of the sequence of vocal-verbal sound units (which can be recorded more acutely and fully by an instrument than by our auditory system), and the psychic aspect consists of the feeling tone and/or intention of the speaker as experienced by us (which no instrument is capable of recording), the two aspects being given in and with each other.

Although, as a rule, the insights regarding the enduring properties (stamps) of a personality that are derived from vocal-verbal psychoids are more revealing than those derived from motor psychoids, the collection of personological data of this sort was not, as I have said, among the author's aims; and consequently he did not have this special reason for devoting a relatively larger amount of space to verbal psychoids. Furthermore, the detailed study of verbal psychoids, with all their subtle nuances and ambiguities of tone, style, meaning, and purpose, could be more feasibly undertaken after the simpler motor psychoids had been systematically examined, as reported in the publication that we have at hand. This having been the wiser decision at the given time, the moving pictures shown to Professor From's experimental subjects were unaccompanied by sound; that is, the motor actions of the portrayed person were not complicated by the occurrence of any speech sequences (verbal psychoids).

Another large class of *psychoids* are behavior traces: things—such as footprints, material artifacts, or written documents—produced by a then-absent human being (known or unknown, living or dead), which are coupled in our experiencing of them with one or more psychic entities (e.g., the state of mind, aim, or intellectual powers of the producer of the observed traces, whoever he might have been).

The psychoid concept is central to the author's thesis. In fact a large part of the intriguing enterprise that is so amply recorded in this volume could well be viewed as a keen and unremitting search for varieties of psychoid entities experienced by normal, younger or older adults in everyday Western life. This is a consciousness-expanding endeavor which each one of us could independently undertake for his own benefit by moving about in the world and noting in detail the nature and value of the yield (i.e., the immediately given outcome of the sensory processing) of different psychoid entities, as well as the apparent or possible determinants thereof.

In following the author's quest for psychoids it is important to remember that in the episodes with which he is concerned, the observer and the observed are not engaged in a face-to-face transaction. The observer (any one of us or an experimental subject) is a detached *witness* of behavior which has no bearing on his own existence and hence calls for no overt response from him. That is to say, in this treatise experiencing other people does not include experiencing the people with whom the experiencer has become interactionally involved and does not include the people whose expressive or purposive behavior sequences are directed toward him; and therefore no occasions are presented here for considering any of the varieties of the most influential species of intuitions: intuitions of self-reference (e.g., "She loves me—she loves me not"; "He's for me—he's against me"; "He looks up to me—he looks down on me.").

Although Professor From does not deal with the question of the validity of a witness's experiences (intuitions) of the covert mental aspect of an actor's overt situational transactions, he does record a number of the least debatable determinants of the nature, abundance, or presumptive value of intuitions of this sort. The following examples should suffice: (1) the general or specific releasiveness of the given or selected situation, that is, its power to activate and release (bring forth) exhibitions or expressions of one or more major dispositions, generally from a variety of personalities, or specifically from a certain type of personality; and (2) the general or specific self-expressiveness of the actor, that is, the extent to which one or more of his major dispositions are both activated and revealed (voluntarily or involuntarily exhibited or expressed), generally in a variety of situations, or specifically in a certain class of situations. The combination of these two factors determines in part the quantity and quality of what will be made available for processing by the nonparticipating witness.

Some other determinants of the outcome and validity of the experiencing process reside in the observer: for example (3) the observer's familiarity with the nature of the physical or social situation in which the actor is involved (e.g. the customary use of each of the encountered objects, the cultural "demands" of the occasion, etc.); and (4) the observer's knowledge of the personality (e.g., action potentials, style) of the actor, or, more generally, of actors of that age, sex, nationality, status, vocation, type, etc. Generally speaking, one expects an actor in a familiar situation to act as other people act conventionally, or to act pretty much as he has acted in the past, though in recent years (since World War II) many of us have learnt to anticipate less social conformity and less self-conformity than was prevalent in earlier times. In some quarters novelty and change have become the rule. Intuitions regarding mental entities in the head of the actor are not necessarily involved in the arousal of such expectations. The observer merely experiences (imagines) what action (material sequence) will be perceived next, that is, what the actor is "about to do." The simplest prospections (involuntary predictions) of this nature are no doubt susceptible of explanation by reference to the registration and retention in the brain mind of frequently and/or recently perceived sequences of events (laws of temporal integration and Pavlovian conditioning). The sound of the dinner bell, say, excites in the actor images of food-to-be-had and in the detached observer images of the actor's habitual overt reaction to the bell. If, as expected, the actor stops what he is doing, the observer's prospective imagery will be experienced as a surmise (a hypothesis, assumption, prediction, or even certainty) that the actor will go (at once or a little later) to the dinner table and start eating, etc.

The following are among other possible partial determinants or modifiers of the way in which the behavior of other people is experienced and described: (5) the available vocabulary or preferred conceptual representors stored in the head of the observer: we perceive and apperceive what we have words for, and sometimes what our theories call for; (6) the enduring cognitive type or momentary cognitive attitude of the observer: some persons are consistently inclined or become temporarily set to focus on one or another aspect (say, on the material or the mental aspect) of the behavior sequences produced by another person; and (7) the existing hedonic, emotional, or wantful state of the observer, which, in some instances, may result in his experiencing, among other possible things, a comparable dispositional state in the mind of the actor.

Professor From does not deal with the difficult question of how to account for the fact that all of us are to a varying extent disposed to "experience," in ways that the author does not identify for us precisely, one or more of the psychological states or processes which a person we are watching may (or may not) be subjectively experiencing. Stated in this way, the term "experience" might suggest phenomena such as those of (presumptively) feeling the feelings of other people, or feeling as one would feel if one were in the shoes of another person and as situationally involved and reactive as he appears to be—phenomena which have called for the invention of such terms as empathy, unconscious identification or imitation, introjection, and so forth. But since this complex topic, germane as it may be, is not within the author's circumference of discourse, I shall not wrestle with it here. The phenomena that are at the focus of Professor From's attention are not the observer's internal kinesthetic sensations, feelings, imaginations, or sympathetically felt hopes as introspectively identified but the feelings, wants, and aims that the observer extrospectively and believingly attributes to the person he is watching. Insofar as these beliefs are congruent with actual current happenings in that other person's mind, the observer's knowledge and understanding of what "makes the man tick" has been increased or reconfirmed. This means that Professor From's work belongs—as I think he would agree—in the domain of cognition, or, more exactly, in a subregion of that domain devoted to the study of what true or false momentary beliefs about the psychological experiences of others are involuntarily arrived at in everyday life merely by observing their behavior with our instrumentally unaided senses.

A serious ambiguity in the use of the term "experience" becomes most obvious here when we are speaking, on the one hand (as Professor From does), of our "experiencing" (in a cognitive sense) the actor's intention to do a certain thing, and, on the other hand, of the actor's "experiencing" (in a conative sense) his own intention to do that thing. One solution might be to retain the latter usage since it conforms more closely to the usual meaning of the word, and to eliminate ambiguity by speaking of our experiencing perceptions of the actor's material behavior sequences and simultaneously experiencing intuitions as to the imperceptible intentions that are guiding the direction of that behavior, the assumption being that such intuitions occur so rapidly (a fraction of a second) after the perceptions that the two processes are experienced by us as an inseparable unity, "in and with" each other. With the maturing of the cognitive system, however, one gains the power to disunite the two processes when necessary, to distinguish between what we have seen another person do as a matter of fact and whatever intuitions (guesses, surmises, imaginations, inferences) we have been offered regarding the doer's motivating forces, wants, purposes, aims, stamps, and so on.

At this point I hope that I may be indulgently allowed a few speculative proposals as partial explanations of the occurrence of intuitions of this sort. My first proposal is that the practice of immediately and involuntarily attributing to another person some namable psychological state or process is demonstrative of a general subconscious assumption (inherent faith) that the ongoing life of other human beings is marked by covert conscious experiences similar to our own, or, more specifically, by experiences of distinguishable subjective states, processes, and representors (image, words) comparable to those which we have experienced ourselves, introspectively discriminated, and named (initially according to the labels we received in childhood from our parents). My second proposal is that this universally shared subconscious assumption is the product of an in-built potential disposition (with countless previous generations of survival value) whose operation has been positively reinforced in us by innumerable successes dating from the dawn of consciousness: for example, by having our apperceptions of psychological states (e.g., fatigue, sorrow, anger) in other people confirmed by their avowals of such states. In short, attributing certain familiar kinds of psychic entities to others—despite billions of resultant errors, misunderstandings, and pathological delusions—has paid off (statistically speaking) in the long run. My third proposal is that the exercise of this involuntary process has paid off (proved advantageous, generally speaking, to members of the human species), primarily because the kinds of psychic entities which are thereby ascribed to other people are almost always those which are experienced by us as determinants of their behavior (e.g., emotions, wants, intentions, executives of intentions), and because these ascribed psychic determinants of behavior are more often congruent than incongruent with the actual determinants, and therefore, by and large, they have both explanatory and predictive value. In other words, the disposition to rapidly attribute psychic forces of this nature to another person has persisted in the human mind because it constitutes the basis for a realistic anticipation of what that person will be doing or trying to do next or somewhat later, an anticipation which often benefits the anticipator by providing him with enough time to adjust to what is coming, or, in certain critical situations (e.g., the murderous intention of an enemy, the suicidal intention of a friend), just enough time to forestall disaster.

Of all the single terms, or concepts, that we have in psychology to refer to one or another variable that is involved in determining the course of a unit of overt behavior, none is more powerful than the concept of *intention* (a variety of *sens*). To be granted a valid hunch as to an actor's ongoing intention is usually to be most aided in anticipating what he will *end* by doing, as well as in explaining what he is *now* doing (in terms of its service to the accomplishment of the intended end). But is this language as clear and unambiguous as it should be? Let us judge. In conformity with the author's usage, *Webster's Dictionary* defines intention as a "determination to do a specified thing or act in a specified way," which means, first of all, that a more or less specific imaginal representation—say, a fantasy or idea—of something which might be done in the immediate or more distant future must be composed in the mind, rapidly or gradually, before a determination can become established to do that specified thing. If the imagined, intended action is a simple, often-executed, effort-producing movement, such as inspiring tobacco smoke (Professor From's favorite example), the whole process of establishing an intention may occur in a fraction of a second at the margin of consciousness.

But representations of intended acts are not usually limited to those that the actor would presumptively end by executing; they are likely to include a rough progression of imagined instrumental, or subsidiary, acts (subintentions, subeffects) which might constitute the preliminary phase leading up to the main, terminal phase of a unitary span of effective motor movements. Under some circumstances, a more perfect coordination of the motor movements themselves (e.g., learning, improving, or rehearsing a technical skill) becomes the object of a conscious intention (cf. an intention to "act in a specified way"). But, ordinarily, neither Professor From nor the Behaviorists since Watson specify an action by describing the pattern of motor movements which produces the observed effect.

In one of the moving pictures shown to the author's subjects a man is seen sitting at a desk, and later reaching out and grasping a pipe (at which point an onlooking subject may surmise that he is intending to smoke—what else does one do with a pipe?). This surmise is sustained when the man fetches some tobacco and packs it into the bowl of his pipe. Then he is seen putting his hand into his pocket; and now the observer is likely to experience or intuit (or attribute to the actor) an intention (subintention) to fetch a match and light his pipe (to produce this subeffect), the observer having previously concluded that the man's intended and expectantly satisfying, terminal thing to do was to smoke his pipe. This array of concrete facts illustrates, I hope, the utility, if not the necessity, of the concept of subintention, since the subordinate (subsidiary, instrumental) acts which constitute the preliminary phase are *not* unintended and it is important to distinguish these subintentions from the superordinate (dominant) intention which accounts for their existence and which, if ultimately actualized, will bring a whole unit of behavior to a close.

One more point: the intention to do something portrayed in the imagination must be distinguished from the actual *doing* of that thing. In Professor From's studies of short and simple action sequences, there is no apparent necessity of making this distinction, since one can depend not only on the persistence of whatever intention is established at the start of each of them (the psychic aspect reported by the observer) but on the power (the will and the muscle-governing ability) of the actor (a psychic aspect *not* reported by the observer) to execute the intended action sequence (the material aspect reported by the observer). Consequently, in such cases, we can assume for practical purposes that the idea of an intended action is enough to bring about its overt actualization (cf. the ideo-motor theory). But a larger view informs us that a person may entertain (1) fantasies of action which he never seriously resolves to execute; (2) fantasies which become goal-oriented plans of action which he resolves to execute some time in the future but never does execute; (3) plans which he endeavors (strives) to execute but without success; and (4) plans which he executes successfully. Here the word "plan" may be applied to the momentary mental representation of a very short, easily executed act (e.g., opening a window) or to an enduring representation of a very long series of intended actions which can be successfully executed only by great efforts and some newly acquired skills. What we need here I would say, what I am fumbling for, is a more suitable, more usable term than volition and willing or conation and striving to refer to the psychic force that is operating whenever the "I" of the actor is consciously and voluntarily actuating his muscles and directing them (with the aid of feedback loops) toward the production of a preconceived and specified situational effect. At such times he is executing or actualizing a plan of action; but we never say this, Professor From does not say this. What we habitually say is that he is *doing* a specified thing—first, he is filling his pipe (with the intention of smoking), and later he is smoking. Filling his pipe and smoking are the perceptible material aspects of two spans of activity, during the first of which we don't hesitate to attribute an intention (psychic entity) to the actor; but during the second span when he is actually executing his initial intention, we do not specifically refer to any accompanying psychic entity. It seems, however, that we must be subconsciously assuming all along that *he* is *the* active agent, the governor of his muscles, and hence responsible for the effects which he compels them to produce for him. The actor might be saying to himself: "I will, therefore I am," and maybe "will" is still the best word we have today for the action-governing entity in the brain-mind. If it is, we should be inventing or searching for a better one.

Table of Contents

Introduction

OTHER PEOPLE AND THEIR BEHAVIOR are becoming dominant themes in psychology—partly as a reaction to the former dominating interest in the individual and his mental life.

I have made an attempt here to throw some light on a number of questions connected with the problem of what happens when we observe or experience the behavior of others. I aim to call attention to certain aspects of the phenomenology of human behavior, to investigate and describe the topics within the world of everyday life with which we are dealing when we ordinarily talk about experiencing others and their behavior.

First let me stress that I am here using the words "others" and "behavior" in such a way that they refer to something which is given purely phenomenologically, i.e., in the content of the experience itself. I am limiting myself to the experienced data, just as within other areas of the psychology of perception we investigate color, figures, temperatures, etc., as they appear in the experience of the observer, differentiating sharply between what exists in the experience and what in some way or other can be said to exist from the point of view of physics and to influence our sense organs.

In order to understand my problem it is of the greatest importance to distinguish between two things: on the one hand, we have the person as he appears in our experience, the experienced person, with his behavior and characteristics as they manifest themselves in our experience, his experienced behavior, his experienced characteristics; and, on the other hand, the—in some scientific sense of the words—"factually existing" person and his—in some scientific sense—"factually existing" behavior and characteristics.

As far as the "factual" characteristics and behavior of other people are concerned, psychologists have taken a great interest in these topics and have investigated them from different points of view and in different ways—using behavioristic and other methods. This book is not concerned with these topics: it does not deal with the question of how others, in some sense of the word, "factually" are, but with the question of how they manifest themselves in our experience. Consequently I am not discussing the question of how to ascertain the "factual" nature of other people.

It is as if psychological research has omitted a link in the chain and tended to operate with a kind of "objective behavior," independent of the observer, while very little has been made of the investigation of the structure of our *experience* of others and of their behavior, and of the laws to be discerned within this area.

Because we simply see what people do, and because the experience of intention and purpose is not the result of a conscious process of deduction from the events we perceive but is something immediately apparent, it has been possible to make the peculiar mistake of regarding behavior with its inherent purpose as something belonging to a sphere of objective facts. And in making this mistake, which might be called the "behavioristic fallacy," the important task of elucidating how we experience behavior has in my opinion been grossly neglected.

Now it seems to me that a phenomenological unraveling of these problems is really not only a useful but an essential preparation before proceeding to investigate not how we experience others but how others in some sense "factually" are, since our actual experience of others often forms the point of departure for such investigations.

As mentioned before I will concern myself solely with this preliminary investigation. I will limit myself to the data present in the experience, in exactly the same way in which in the study of the psychology of perception we investigate the experienced colors without taking any interest in the electromagnetic waves, factually existing from the point of view of physical science.

(To state the problem in this way leads to certain linguistic difficulties. Usually when we talk about experiencing the behavior of others, we assume that this behavior in some sense or other exists independent of the observer as perceiving individual. To maintain the distinction set out above, I ought not to say "the experience of the behavior of others," or "experiencing others" but "the experience of that which manifests itself for us as the behavior of others" and a whole row of similarly laborious and lengthy formulations.) Such expressions would have weighed very heavily on the exposition and obscured the meaning. I have therefore chosen to use the ordinary expressions from our everyday language and to leave it to the reader to remember the overall intention. Consequently, when I talk about the experience of the mental characteristics, intentions, feelings, etc., of others, I mean: the experience of that which manifests itself to us as the mental characteristics, intentions, feelings, etc., of others.

I have aimed at writing the treatise in the straightforward language of everyday life, as it is my belief that psychology in general, and the field with which I am concerned in particular, is as yet insufficiently developed scientifically to warrant the employment of a special technical terminology. The greater precision which would result from such a procedure would easily be of a nature which only the author and those of his readers who have approximately the same background would enjoy, while running the risk that for all others the idea would be obscured rather than elucidated. It will take a long time before psychology possesses a precise, generally accepted terminology. For the time being I think it would be advantageous as far as possible to use the language of everyday life when dealing with problems such as those with which this treatise is concerned.

I have tried to treat the problems partly by using experimental investigations and partly by gathering such observations from everyday life and from more special areas of life as would be useful in elucidating my problems. I hope I have succeeded in making the different methods supplement and support each other.

I also hope that my results may be of interest not only to psychologists but to teachers, physicians, clergymen, lawyers, and others who in their work are concerned with the description and evaluation of men. I believe that the subject can be of interest to sociologists, since the way in which we experience each other of necessity must influence relationships between people.

1 ∗ Two Aspects of Perceived Behavior

Let me begin with a very ordinary and minor situation from everyday life. I see a man putting his hand into the pocket of his trousers to get his matches, after he has just placed a cigarette between his lips. I do not see—and only if I had a very special mental set or attitude would I be able to see—that he moves his hand down along the thigh, then slightly upward in under the edge of his coat and finally downward again into the pocket. What I see is that he puts his hand into the pocket to get his matches.

If we confine ourselves to such a common experience of the behavior of another person, then the meaning or purpose of the act of behavior is intrinsic to the perception of the behavioral sequence, i.e., the movements of the hand and arm. We see what people *intend* by the actions they are executing. If I see a young lady look at her face in the mirror and then produce her powder compact, then I see immediately that she means to powder herself; when she stops with the puff suspended in mid-air, then I see that she is wondering whether the nose needs yet another pat or whether it has had enough. If I consider the matter afterward, it is possible that I would regard some of the things I saw as signs of mental processes; generally this does not happen while I am actually observing the situation. The sign and that which is signified are fused together and do not appear as two separate entities in my actual perception of the action. The material sequence and the intentions, purpose, ideas, thoughts, and considerations which I perceive in the person are all given in and with each other, in my perception of the action of the other person.

It is far from always true to say that the intentions, purposes, etc., which are given intrinsically with the material sequence appear clearly and distinctly in my experience of the behavior of another. I may perceive these psychological states in a very clear and distinct way, but very often they are only vaguely present in my perception of the other person. I see that the man is lighting his cigarette, and if I assume a particular set, his intention appears quite clearly: I see the young lady attend to her make-up, and if I interest myself further in her behavior, her deliberations appear quite clearly in my experience of her. On the other hand, if I do not take any particular interest in the other person but only perceive his behavior casually, then his psychological state will only be present in a more casual way. Something mental is present, but only in an extremely vague and imprecise fashion. The experience has been mentally processed, as it were, at a low level and only after we have altered our set (or *Einstellung*) do we process it to a higher degree, so that the intention, for example, of the other person is included in our perception of his behavior. However, in a number of cases it does happen that the mental life of the observed person appears in our experience, not because we are set to perceive it but because the behavioral situation, as we experience it, has certain characteristics in itself which result in the manifestation of the mental life of the other. This question will be treated in detail in Chapter 4.

I stated that the experienced material sequence and the intentions, purposes, and deliberations which I experience in the acting person are given "in and with" each other. The mental aspect, e.g., an intention, is so closely intertwined with the material sequence—the movements the person executes with his body, limbs, and facial muscles—that it is generally extremely difficult to distinguish the two sides of the perceived totality separately from each other. Considering the event later and attempting to describe the two aspects apart, it will usually be easy to describe the mental aspect. The truth of the matter is that we describe behavior, in the main, by indicating the psychological states of the subject which form a part of our perception of the behavior—and not by describing the material sequence itself. It is generally extremely difficult to carry such a description through. Only rarely in our perception do we separate each of the movements which occur when we experience the actions of someone else. For example, I have often seen a man put his hand into his pocket to get his matches, but only a rather detailed analysis of the occurrence revealed to me that the movements forming this simple act depend on whether the man wears a single- or double-breasted coat and whether the coat is buttoned up or is hanging open.

Let me sum up: When we have to describe a behavior sequence, we generally do so by indicating a perception of some psychological state in the behaving person. A good example of how this can be the case even when the material sequences involved are not performed by either human beings or animals can be found in an investigation carried out by Fritz Heider and Marianne Simmel.[1] Their subjects were shown a short film sequence, lasting about 2-½ minutes. The sequence showed a circle, together with a large and a small triangle, which all moved in various ways. *Inter alia* the film was shown to 34 subjects who were instructed to write down what happened in the film; this was done in order to investigate how many subjects would see the figures as living beings. Nearly everybody did see them in this way. There was only one subject who gave a description nearly exclusively in terms of geometry. All the other subjects described the movements of the figures as the behavior of living beings, in most cases of human beings, but in two cases as movements of birds. Later the film was shown to 36 subjects who were instructed to interpret the movements of the figures as those of human beings—and all 36 obeyed the instructions. They said that the figures fight each other, avoid each other, approach each other, and so on. This way of describing the movements of the figures seems surprisingly obvious and con-

[1] Fritz Heider and Marianne Simmel, "An Experimental Study of Apparent Behavior," *Amer. J. Psychol.,* 57 (1944), 245.

vincing, while a purely "geometrical" description gives a very hazy understanding of the sequence. As a result the authors of the paper find themselves forced to use certain anthropomorphic expressions when they are describing the film sequence to the readers, because a purely geometrical description would be too involved and too difficult to understand.

If we are concerned not with movements of triangles but with the behavior of men and women, it becomes extremely difficult to describe the behavior sequences without the use of expressions concerned with the mental aspects, which are given in our experience of the subject's actions. However, an attempt has of course been made: Watson wanted, he says, to create a purely objective psychology by not considering consciousness. "The time seems to have come when psychology must discard all reference to consciousness; when it need no longer delude itself into thinking that it is making mental states the objects of observation." [2] But when Watson then attempts to describe human behavior without "any reference to consciousness," it happens time after time that he uses just those expressions which have to do with the mental aspects of the experienced behavior; the ghost of consciousness is not so easily exorcised. As Rubin put it: "Those of the behaviorists who formulate their descriptions not in the terms of the three-dimensional coordinates of the world of physics, but in terms of behavior escape the difficulties of their theoretical position when they smuggle the mental aspect into their descriptions by the use of this kind of psychoid entities." [3]

Wolfgang Köhler also noticed the problem and expressed his surprise when in the writings of Watson he found descriptions of the behavior of infants involving, for example, goal-directedness of the observed movements. [4]

[2] John B. Watson, "Psychology as the Behaviorist Views It," *Psychol. Rev.*, 20 (1913), 163.

[3] Edgar Rubin, "Bemerkungen über unser Wissen von anderen Menschen," *Experimenta Psychologica* (Copenhagen, 1949), p. 32.

[4] Wolfgang Köhler, *Gestalt Psychology* (New York, 1929), p. 252.

A couple of examples will show how mental aspects can intrude themselves into even the most behaviorist accounts. In the well-known investigations of the emotions of the infant there is a description of the reactions of the nine-month-old Albert after the experimenter on several occasions had placed a rat close to the child and then, when he was engrossed in the animal, banged on a steel bar behind him: "Rat presented suddenly without sound. There was steady fixation but no tendency at first to reach for it. The rat was then placed nearer, whereupon tentative reaching movements began with the right hand. When the rat nosed the infant's left hand, the hand was immediately withdrawn. He started to reach for the head of the animal with the forefinger of the left hand, but withdrew it suddenly before contact." [5] After Albert had acquired a fear of the rat, an investigation was made of his reactions to cotton wool. "The wool was presented in a paper package. At the end the cotton was not covered by the paper. . . . He then began to play with the paper, avoiding contact with the wool itself." [6] And later, when the boy was exposed to a fur coat, the following is a part of the description of his reaction: "Again there was the strife between withdrawal and the tendency to manipulate. Reached tentatively with left hand but drew back before contact had been made." [7]

The examples show that all the time certain goals and intentions are given also in Watson's perception of the reaction of infants—in the one case he even perceives a conflict between two intentions in the behavior of the child.

This is the way we do perceive behavior. And if we observe an infant struggling in vain to put his finger into his mouth, then the purpose of the action is intrinsic to the groping movements which we see, and this to such an extent that an attempt to describe the material sequence without stating the purpose would be extremely

---

[5] John B. Watson and Rosalie Rayner, "Conditioned Emotional Reactions," *J. Exp. Psychol.*, 3 (1920), 4.
[6] *Ibid.*, p. 7.   [7] *Ibid.*, p. 10.

difficult. Even the keenest follower of Watson, wishing to describe the behavior of infants from a "thoroughly objective viewpoint," has hardly any other way to do so than the following: Subject S . . . attempted for 15 minutes to get her finger in her mouth, but did not succeed." [8] Here an attempt to "give a description in the three-dimensional coordinates of physics," without considering intention or purpose, would be very involved. You do find several behaviorists who have given up the struggle to exterminate these descriptions and instead they speak, as E. C. Tolman does, about "purposive behavior," saying that "motive, intention, determining set and the like" can be observed in the behavior of living beings without necessarily talking about consciousness and conscious life.[9]

Thus, an attempt to give a description of the isolated material sequence appears to run into considerable difficulties when we are dealing with experienced behavior. Even Watson, who was directly interested in carrying through such an attempt, has not managed the exercise in a very convincing manner, while Tolman and others take exception to the original teaching on just this point.

Now, with regard to the other side of perceived behavior, the side we have called the mental aspect, we find as I have already stated that the ordinary description of a behavior sequence includes the purpose or intention of the action. This is perhaps seen most clearly if we try to describe action without quite knowing the meaning of that action. In such cases it may well happen that we attempt to describe the material sequence but often the description will consist exactly in a search for the purpose: he stood and moved the hand around as if he were looking for something; he swung his arms about as if he were chasing a bee; and so on.

Now, while it seems quite straightforward to describe the behavior of others by an indication of the purpose of the action as it

[8] Margaret G. Blanton, "The Behavior of the Human Infant During the First Thirty Days of Life," *Psychol. Rev.*, 24 (1917), 478.

[9] See E. C. Tolman, "A New Formula for Behaviorism," *Psychol. Rev.*, 29 (1922), 44–53.

appears to us, this does not mean to say that the purpose is identified perceptually as something separate, something which exists independently in some fashion "behind" or in some other way independent of the movements seen. In the perception itself there is no dualism. Normally we do not experience other people as consisting of body plus mind.

This is related to the point which Rubin makes, in the paper cited above, that in everyday life we rarely apply Descartes' sharp division between mind and matter in anything like a consistent manner. If we analyze such experienced entities as, let us say, a friendly smile, then we discover that they are different from a lot of other entities; one apparent way of describing the difference is to say that these entities have a mental aspect in addition to the material. But this difference is not present to everyday perception.

Rubin says:

Here we meet entities which are quite undifferentiated ("einheitlich"), and they do not appear as a mixture of something mental and something material. They correspond to entities in the scientific sense that explicitly refer to something which is at one and the same time mental and material. These entities are originally undifferentiated in the same sense as the timbre of a tone is an undifferentiated phenomenon, as pointed out by Cornelius, for example. This phenomenon does not consist of harmonics, but a change of attitude or set will make possible the transformation of the phenomenon, without any change in the stimulus; it then becomes possible to hear individual overtones. Such entities, which by adopting another set can be replaced by others also consisting of both material and mental components, we shall call *psychoid entities*.[10]

These experienced entities appear not as something mental and something material: the two aspects are given in and with each other. But when we first begin to study the problem, then we can grasp both these aspects of the totality. We can establish that such perceptions have both a mental and a bodily aspect. Rubin maintains that with a different set we can replace these entities by others

[10] "Bemerkungen über unser Wissen von anderen Menschen," p. 32.

consisting of material and mental components; if this means that it should be possible in some way to separate the two from each other so that we have the mental component by itself and the bodily component by itself, then I am unable to agree completely with Rubin. It seems to me to be extremely difficult when I see a friendly face to arrive by a change in set at a new entity where the mental friendliness is perceived by itself and the face as something entirely material by itself. But perhaps we can simply understand Rubin to mean that he thinks it possible to state that the friendly face has two aspects—but not to say that it would be possible afterward to distinguish between them except that we can take more interest first in one aspect, then in the other.

Human movements which we experience are very often this kind of psychoid entity. Rubin states that they are psychoid entities as soon as we experience them as actions and therefore see them as having a purpose, while he does not include movements which cannot be experienced as actions. "Certain kinds of nervous tics, for example, are simply bodily movements and not actions, and they are very noticeable precisely because they are meaningless (that is, without mental components)." [11] However, in most cases it will be more practical to include such movements, e.g., nervous tics, with what Rubin has called psychoid entities. It is true that they are perceived as meaningless in the sense that the person has no purpose in doing them; he does not intend to make them. But if we analyze the experience afterward, it will usually be the case that the "absence of meaning" is actually a mental aspect, in some ways similar to the purpose we experience if we see the movements as a purposeful action.

When we investigate the problem, we find that such meaningless movements, on the one hand, are of the same class as what we could call the expressive movements, such as smiles, creases in the forehead, tearful crying, yawns from boredom, laughter. The movements which enter into these behavior patterns are not determined by a purpose—the person does not intend to make them; but the

[11] *Ibid.*

mental aspect in the experience of these movements can be very obvious indeed. Nervous tics are often perceived as the person appearing nervous, restless, anxious, afraid of being exposed, or other such traits, and whenever this is the case the movements are to be regarded as expressive movements.

In other cases the "meaningless" aspect can be the dominant one and then the perception is more reminiscent of what we perceive in situations where we do not understand the meaning of the behavior of another person. Then the movements are not perceived as expressions of anything but as a special kind of action which has the particular property that the purpose is not present in our experience. On the contrary: The "absence of meaning" is a dominant aspect and gives the experienced behavior a very special flavor. In extreme cases we tend to describe such behavior as abnormal.

A small example will clarify this point. One afternoon when Professor Rubin and I had already put on our overcoats, ready to go home from the laboratory, Rubin said: "See here, From." At the same moment he sat down at his desk and looked straight ahead while he made short abrupt horizontal movements right and left in the air in front of him with his right hand, keeping the index finger and the thumb closely together. I just managed to think something like "What on earth has happened to Rubin," when he got hold of a pencil and a piece of paper, drew a system of small arrows and pushed the paper across to me, saying: "Here is the code to the safety lock on my bicycle. Would you mind riding the bike home for me?" The earlier perception of something completely incomprehensible was immediately replaced, and the purpose of his behavior, i.e., to note down the code which he "had in his fingers," became quite apparent and was formulated more or less in words such as: "Oh, that was the idea."

Later we shall discuss certain problems in connection with the fact that at times we do perceive the behavior of others as meaningless. But before we proceed with the argument, let us first have a closer look at the entities which Rubin called psychoid entities and try to sketch an outline of the field to which they belong.

2 * The Varieties of Psychoid Entities

Our perceptions of the things around us have a great number of properties and qualities which do not have the characteristics of sense qualities. Frequently these properties are intrinsic to the experience of the sense qualities, so that it is only by subsequent analysis of the experience that we can separate them, while in other instances these qualities may be given in a more or less indirect fashion.

In most cases, when we perceive something, we perceive at the same time what this something is. "Perceiving an object we are also aware of the nature of the object," says Frithiof Brandt.[1] Our perceptions are subsumed under certain more or less definite headings. We shall discuss these problems in more detail in Chapter 3.[2] Looking at a thing, we can see how it will react in certain situations: a glass will splinter, a string will burst, a smile will disappear, under the appropriate circumstances. We experience more or less directly what things are capable of, what powers they have; we see, with Locke, that fire can melt, that sun can bleach.[3] And many things appear with what Rubin has called a "utility determination." We see immediately that a hammer is meant for hammering, a pencil for writing, a pipe for smoking. Further, there are many objects

---

[1] Frithiof Brandt, *Psykologi,* 3rd ed. (Copenhagen, 1947), II, 29.

[2] On the question of this subsuming, see also Franz From, *Drøm og neurose* (*Dream and Neurosis*), 2nd ed. (Copenhagen, 1951), pp. 8–14.

[3] These qualities which Locke calls "secondary qualities, mediately perceived," and of which he says that they are usually called "powers," would generally fall within the area of which we are now speaking—in contradistinction to his "secondary qualities, immediately perceived" among which he counts such things as color, taste, smell, etc. (John Locke, *An Essay Concerning Human Understanding,* Book II, Chap. VIII, paragraphs 23–26).

which we experience immediately as beautiful, others as ugly. Frequently we see whether an object is fashioned by human hands or whether it is a "natural object." We may also mention the fact that things hang together in our experience; they are related to each other in innumerable ways.

Among all the experienced entities which appear to us devoid of the characteristics of sense qualities, the psychoid entities form an area which is fairly easily distinguishable from the others. In most of the above examples we find that the qualities which do not possess the imprint of sense qualities have to do with a knowledge in the observer, so that they can in some way be said to have a mental aspect. If, for example, I see a cup, then my experience of it as intended for drinking may be intrinsic to the sight of the cup. This "determination of utility" may in some cases be immediately present as a property of the cup. A short consideration will easily persuade me that the immediately experienced quality is dependent on the knowledge I have of the object, i.e., on something mental.

There seems, however, to be a rather obvious difference between such experiences as seeing that a cup is meant for drinking and seeing that a man is happy. And the difference is one we wish to stress: in the latter case the mental aspect of the experienced entity has to do with something mental outside myself. Normally, the mental aspect of a psychoid entity has something to do with the psychological state in another person; in other cases with some psychological state of an animal; and yet in other cases with some quasi-psychological state in a thing. It is possible, however, to perceive psychoid entities where the psychical aspect has to do with a mental quality in ourselves. This is so when we perceive ourselves as an external object. It is more reminiscent of the perception of another person, as for example when I perceive my face in the mirror and note that "I really look happy" or when I notice that my hand is shaking and think that "I am really nervous" or again when I read something I have written myself and experience what it says in the text, the meaningfulness of the passage, and the like.

Tentatively we can now limit our area of inquiry by calling entities that have a material as well as a mental aspect psychoid entities, provided the mental aspect has to do either with something mental or mental-like outside ourselves or with something of the mental aspect of ourselves but seen as it were from without. Within the area defined in this way we have several groups of perceived entities.

First, there is the direct perception of others as they are present to us in our daily encounters. Second, we may include the entities which we perceive as the results of actions. Third, we may include the psychoid entities which are present in the language. And finally, there is a fourth group in which we include the psychoid entities where the mental aspect has nothing to do with something mental in a human being.

1. The Direct Experience of Others

The first group includes actions by our fellow man. The mental aspect is here a purpose, intention, meaning, or similar "directing factor." There are also emotional expressions where the mental aspect is an actual psychological condition. Finally, we have the psychoid entities where the mental characteristics such as character and intelligence are given in and with something material; this special form of expression, which we very often find it difficult to distinguish from emotional expressions, we shall call a "stamp."

ACTIONS

In discussing actions we shall take the word in the widest possible sense and include all experienced entities where the mental aspect has an appearance of being purposive—where we experience that the person has a meaning in his behavior. It can be an "action element" as when we see a person reach for something, look for something, follow after or avoid something; or it can be a short, more or less independent, self-contained action pattern, as when we see someone smoke a cigarette, eat a meal, read a book, or conduct a conversation.

When we experience such actions, we normally observe a part of the material sequence only; but often the whole of the action can be present nevertheless in our experience. The reason is that the perceived sequence in some way refers to a more complete sequence. If we see the beginning of the action only, the whole of the action can appear to us as inherent in the sequence which we see. If I see a man pour himself a glass of beer and drink a mouthful, then I can perceive that he is drinking a glass of beer. Inherent in the perception of an element of the sequence is the perception of the whole sequence.

With E. Tranekjær Rasmussen [4] we shall say that a part of the sequence can be the manifest form of the whole sequence, or more generally that a short sequence can be the form under which a longer sequence manifests itself, or in the terminology of Tranekjær Rasmussen: The time-elements of the form under which the entity manifests itself are narrower than the time-elements of the entity itself.[5]

It is not only the beginning of a behavior sequence that can be the basis for the perception of a whole sequence; it can be the end or other parts of the sequence. In the example noted above it is the event of the man drinking a mouthful from the glass which can be the element by which the whole sequence "to drink a glass of beer" is perceived; and it does not matter whether it is the first mouthful, a later one, or even the last—unless of course the total situation indicates that he is, for example, drinking one mouthful only.

At times we can experience the behavior of another as being directed toward a goal far in the future and here the actual action will be the form under which a very complex behavior sequence

[4] Edgar Tranekjær Rasmussen, "Undersøgelser over Erkendelsen" (*Investigations of Human Understanding*) (unpublished manuscript, 1938).

[5] *Ibid.*, para 15.

is manifesting itself: We could mention, for example, attempts to gain the goodwill of another person, to make a fortune, to complete long years of study, to create a career, and so on.

The actual action which we perceive can be the basis not only of a more comprehensive perceived sequence but also of other mental topics. Below, when we discuss the next two groups of perceived expression and perceived "stamp," we shall see that inherent in the experience of a behavior sequence there can be present a feeling, an emotion, or some other psychological quality in the acting person; or the action can be the basis whereby more permanent mental qualities are manifested, such as traits of temperament or character. Sometimes it happens that perceived actions more or less directly indicate certain thought processes in the acting person. We may perceive that the other person is thinking of something—realizing something—that there is something he cannot understand, something he knows, something he remembers, something he has forgotten or is considering or is not considering. The way in which the person acts can become the form in which his thought processes manifest themselves.

In later chapters we shall investigate this kind of psychoid entity, i. e., the actions of other people as they appear in our experience, in much greater detail. Now let us look at the other kinds of psychoid entities.

EXPRESSIONS

The next area within this group of direct experience of other people is composed of psychoid entities of the type we call emotional expressions. We may experience others as happy, unhappy, angry, afraid, curious, uncertain, etc., and the perceived psychological quality intrinsic to the material aspect of the perception is best described as an existing mental condition in the subject. I am not only talking about the mental conditions which we normally call emotions. It is also possible to experience the other person as being aware—or not being aware—of certain things. We may perceive, for example, that he has a certain insight into problems, or that he has no insight, or that his understanding is deficient. This kind of psychoid entity forms a continuum with the next kind within the first group, those we have called "stamps," where the mental aspect is a more permanent quality or trait; often it will then be a matter of preference whether we place a psychoid entity in the category "expression" or "stamp." If we perceive that a man is aggressive, then the mental aspect of the perception may have to do with an existing mental condition in him, or it may appear as a quality or a more permanent trait, depending on the whole structure of the experience. But let us now first look at cases where the mental aspect appears to relate to an existing mental condition in the other person.

Here the material aspect of the perception can be the facial expressions, the facial lines and forms in their constant flux. But all the expressive movements play an important role: gesticulations, and positions and movements of the head and the body. The inflection of the voice and the rhythm of breathing are other aspects; we find, for example, that the relationship between the time taken for inhalation and exhalation varies with the emotional condition.[6]

We can experience the emotional condition of another person inherent in a rather brief facial expression. There are, however, rather great differences with regard to how expressive people's faces are, and it is also true that the different emotions are far from equally clear in facial expressions. Experiments with photographs taken while the subject attempted to produce a definite emotion showed that surprise, for example, was perceived by many observers as was intended while there was great uncertainty with regard to despair.[7]

In our everyday perception of the emotions of others, the material aspects of the experience usually include much more than a

[6] Antoinette Feleky, "The Influence of the Emotions on Respiration," *J. Exp. Psychol.*, 1 (1916), 218–41.

[7] Antoinette Feleky, "The Expression of the Emotions," *Psychol. Rev.*, 21 (1914), 33–41.

brief perception of facial expressions. In most cases we are dealing with a definite sequence including several of the expressive movements listed above. This expressive behavior is distinguishable from those patterns of behavior that are perceived as actions because expressive behavior does not appear as guided by a purpose or a meaning, except in the special cases where a person intends to show his feelings. Apart from expressive movements there are a number of factors which may influence the way in which we perceive the emotions of others: the whole of the perceived situation in which the person is embedded plays an important role. If I am present when a man is a target of offensive behavior, it is not necessary for me to study his appearance and behavior in detail to see whether or not he is happy. If an important wish of his comes true, I may quite directly perceive that he does not feel sad. Very often it is the precise circumstances which have given rise to the feelings and emotions which will decide how we perceive the condition of another. Adam Smith stresses that this applies when we sympathize with some one: "Sympathy, therefore, does not arise so much from the view of the passion as from that of the situation which excites it." [8] The same is also true when we do not sympathize with the other person but only observe his feelings in a more objective and detached way.

A person's emotions are generated by certain events, and our perception of the events may influence the way in which his psychological state appears to us. The condition itself results in certain expressive movements, which in turn influence the way we perceive his feelings. And finally, certain impulses to action may be a part of the emotion. It is possible, with Shand, to regard emotions as systems comprising both the feeling-condition and the impulses to action: "'Emotion' for us will connote not feeling abstracted from impulse but feeling with its impulse." [9] The actions which the feelings prompt us to perform can therefore be-

[8] Adam Smith, *The Theory of Moral Sentiments*, 10th ed. (London, 1804), I, 8.
[9] Alexander Shand, *The Foundations of Character* (London, 1914), p. 178.

come the forms under which the emotional condition manifests itself; we see immediately that the fugitive is afraid, that the attacker is angry. In this way an action as a purposive sequence may function as expression because the behavior sequence becomes the form under which the emotional condition with its impulses for action manifests itself.

But in addition to the special case where an action can function as "expression" because of its quality of action, it is also true that a behavior sequence at one and the same time can be perceived as action and as expression. Given in and with the material sequence, we can have two or more mental aspects: a purpose belonging to the sequence as experienced action and an actual mental condition (or more lasting quality) belonging to the sequence as experienced expression (or stamp).

When we perceive a certain behavior sequence as directed by a purpose, then this behavior is in a way fixed in our experience. If it develops in a different way, it is no longer the original action. But this does not at all mean that the sequence is fixed in all details. It would often be possible to execute the action leading to the fulfillment of the intention in several, quite different ways; the behavior sequence can vary and we may yet experience the same action. Such variations in the material sequence which do not influence the experienced purpose or intention may frequently be of importance in deciding which mental condition we are going to experience in the acting person.

A door can be opened in many ways: for example, it can be done impatiently, hesitantly, or angrily. In and with the way in which it is done, in our experience there will often appear an additional mental aspect apart from the intention—perhaps an actual mental condition in the other person; in this case the sequence becomes both action and expression.

Such a dual aspect of human behavior can, then, be present as given in our experience. In this essay we shall limit ourselves to that which is present in the experience and attempt a description and exposition of this element. I regard this description to be not only a useful but a necessary preliminary investigation before we begin to find methods to explore, not how we experience others, but how others really are, e.g., with regard to character and personality.

With the help of such methods it will then be possible to undertake what the behavior of man "really expresses," to attempt to determine the relationship between perceived behavior and measured personality traits. It will be possible to use Jørgen Jørgensen's expression about language, extending it to other behavior sequences, and say that "the behavior has an expressive or symptomatic function." [10] Perhaps it will be possible to go further and find two sets of factors which are both involved in the determination of behavior, corresponding to the duality which is found in the experience. It is with such ideas that Gordon Allport is concerned when he discusses "expressive versus adaptive behavior." In this connection he regards a certain behavior as determined by two sets of tendencies: one set has to do with "adaptive performance," determined by the problem we are attempting to solve; the other set has to do with "expression" and depends on deep-seated determining traits in the personality. [11] But if we say that "expression" is determined by such personality traits, it is necessary to consider that a number of other factors are also influencing and determining the manifest behavior so that the deep-seated traits are masked, as it were, to a greater or lesser extent—and this is exactly what Allport does. [12] But even if such a "masking" is present—because of an acute emotional condition, the traditional demands for the type of behavior involved, the bodily conditions of the person, or his training and occupation—the way in which the action is carried out will often be the form under which the experienced character trait, degree of intelligence, or other mental property

[10] Jørgen Jørgensen, *Psykologi paa biologisk grundlag* (Copenhagen, 1941–46), p. 455.
[11] Gordon Allport, *Personality* (London, 1949), pp. 465 ff.
[12] *Ibid.*, pp. 468–70.

manifests itself, so that we are dealing with a psychoid entity of the type which we have called a "stamp." This is the last type within the group which includes the direct experience of other people as they are given for us in our dealings with them.

STAMP

When we perceive the mental qualities of another, they can be present for us in many different ways. The purpose we perceive a person as having through his actions can be the form under which the more deep-seated traits of the person manifest themselves, especially if, time and again, we experience the same intentions as directing his actions. If a person's actions often appear to us to be aimed at being helpful to others and making them happy, we may experience him as kind and humane. If we frequently perceive that the actions of another person are aimed at avoiding contact with his neighbors, then we experience him as a misanthrope. If we perceive that a man through his actions intends to make gains for himself at the expense of others, then we would often experience him as an egotistic person.

If we get to know a person well, it would in the final analysis be our perception of his actions (or perhaps of the results of his actions) which determines how we perceive his character. We shall discuss later how our perception of the personality of another person is being formed as we get to know him. Apart from special cases, a closer acquaintance would be necessary so that the perceived stamp may be clearly confirmed by our experience of the actions of the person. As far as the first and more immediate impression of the character of another is concerned, as we perceive it in daily commerce with our fellow man, a number of other factors are also of importance—and here the behavior pattern which we mentioned above plays a not unimportant role.

There are many ways in which to drink a beer, cross the street, eat a beefsteak, ask the way, kiss a girl, sharpen a pencil, and so on. As I said, the manner can vary with the emotional condition of the acting person; but it can also vary from person to person. The individual can put his own stamp on the action, as it were; everyone does it in his own way.

To say that a behavior pattern is characteristic of a person does not mean that it is a psychoid entity, a "stamp." It is possible that we immediately recognize a man by his gait and yet we do not thereby necessarily perceive his psychological condition. But we are dealing with psychoid entities if, intrinsic with the gait, we perceive of a man wanting to appear certain of himself but suffering from an inner feeling of uncertainty ("he is a bragging type but there is no substance behind") or if we experience that another person is "stupid and talks too much," drifts with the current, suffers from an inferiority complex, and is pessimistic. The foregoing expressions are taken from an investigation where judgments with regard to personality were made solely on the basis of the way in which people walked (the gait was shown on film in such a way that the faces were invisible and it was not possible to observe the body build of the subjects clearly).[13]

There are many kinds of behavior which can be perceived in this way, i.e., as the form under which the character of the person is manifested. We can perceive that a person gets up from a chair in a determined way, that he has a reliable handshake, that he sits in a prepossessing manner, that he enters through a doorway in a self-deprecating manner, or that he appears shy in his use of the knife and fork.

Now we must remember that different people do not necessarily behave in equally expressive ways. In some individuals it is as if the behavior pattern at all times is dominated by their character;

[13] Werner Wolff, "Involuntary Self-Expression in Gait and Other Movements: An Experimental Study," *Character and Personality,* 3 (1934–35), 332. A part of the paper was originally published in German in a slightly different version, in a volume putting together selections from the answers to a prize essay on the relationship between gait and character. This volume contains many interesting observations and points of view: H. Bogen and O. Lipmann (eds.), "Gang und Charakter," *Z. f. angewandte Psychol.,* Beiheft 58 (1931).

it tells us something about how the man is. In other individuals the behavior pattern reveals but little of the mental aspects. Further, we must notice that while in one person it is perhaps the gait, in particular, which causes our experience of mental aspects, in another it may be the way of eating, in a third the way of entering a room. It may be the individual's way of behaving while shopping, or it may be his way of talking, which is perceived as a stamp. Experiments on the description of persons on the basis of their voices only, heard over a loud speaker, do demonstrate that with certain speakers the voice can provide the material for a very rich and detailed description of character, while in others the description contains far fewer details regarding the character of the speaker.[14]

Perhaps this perception of some people as revealing their character in one particular behavior pattern, while other people reveal it in another pattern, is connected with differences in the degree to which the various types of behavior patterns are influenced by more basic traits—and therefore the degree to which they are to be regarded as "expressions," in Allport's sense of the word.[15] If so, it would be impossible to employ any single test for personality testing. If one test only were used, rich results would be obtained for those individuals whose character expressed itself specifically through the pattern which happened to be investigated but very meager results for others. In order to ensure a reasonable result, a battery of tests should be employed, comprising measures of a large number of expressive patterns so that each individual case is more likely to be investigated within the particular type of behavior which is particularly influenced by his character.

However, it is not only the behavior pattern of the person which can be perceived as stamp; the mental aspects in others can be perceived as intrinsic in a wide range of different things. We have already mentioned that the voice of the individual can be the form

[14] Herta Herzog, "Stimme und Persönlichkeit," *Z. f. Psychol.,* 130 (1933), 343.
[15] *Personality,* p. 471.

under which certain aspects of his character are manifested and it is precisely the timbre of the voice and the way of speaking which to many people is most important for perceiving the psychological traits of other people.

Another important group of patterns are the facial lineaments. A protruding chin often provides the perception of a strong will, while a high forehead may be the basis by which a perception of intelligence is created. Similarly with a stubby nose and an open, confident manner. We may experience faces as indolent, determined, good-humored, unreliable, and so on.

There is something strange about these perceptions. There seems to be some agreement on how people perceive facial expressions as "stamps," but very often it happens that on closer acquaintance the person "behind the face" disproves the original perception. A man may look unintelligent, but we discover upon closer contact that he is far from stupid; another may look very brutal but may prove to be friendly and patient. And even if these experiences of facial expressions as stamp have been disproved on many occasions, they may nevertheless still dominate our experience of new and hitherto unknown persons. Now it is undoubtedly true that if a person is momentarily determined (looks determined), he will put his chin forward; the one who does not understand a thing (looks unintelligent) lowers the lower jaw and lifts the eyebrows; the person who concentrates on a problem (looks thoughtful) contracts the muscles around the eyes and looks fixedly ahead. Certain facial expressions correspond to these specific mental sets in the same way as certain facial expressions correspond to specific emotional attitudes. Possibly it follows from these considerations that a person whose facial structure and expression resemble, for example, that associated with lack of understanding appears unintelligent—and that all the time, under these circumstances, the facial expressions do not become the form under which a specific mental aspect manifests itself but that of a more permanent trait. The same may be the case with those persons whose facial expressions give us the experience of determination, intelligence, brutality, and so on. There are, however, also many other factors which may be of importance; it is not impossible that popular, commercial art and films may be important for the propagation and acceptance of different patterns, as both the drawing and the acting so often follow the socially preponderant ideas of how the face of a hero, a bandit, a sage, or a fool should look.

In an interesting investigation, Egon Brunswick and Lotte Reiter [16] attempted to study some of these problems in greater detail. They worked with outline drawings of faces; a single, egg-shaped line contour, somewhat flattened at the upper end, the eyes drawn as horizontal ovals with a central dot as pupils, with a vertical line indicating the nose and a horizontal line the mouth. By varying the distance between the eyes, the height of the forehead, the level of the mouth, together with the position and the length of the nose, they obtained 189 different variations of such a facial pattern. The experimental subjects perceived the faces as psychoid entities and were able to describe the "persons." Here are examples of such descriptions: "Nice, young, open, good natured, merry, sympathetic, bright"; [17] and about another figure: "Intelligent, energetic. Interested in work. Not too sympathetic as a man. Very tough. Is inconsiderate and egotistical." [18] Systematic investigations of the dependence of the different "qualities of impressions" on the changes made in the patterns demonstrated, among other things, that the position of the mouth was of the greatest importance. In certain patterns a highly placed mouth would give the impression "gay and young" while a mouth in a low position would produce "sad, old, angry." The investigations gave rise to many interesting problems, but it is doubtful whether it is possible to draw any conclusion with regard to our problem. It seems likely that the authors' results were very strongly influ-

---

[16] Egon Brunswick and Lotte Reiter, "Eindruckscharaktere schematisierter Gesichter," *Z. f. Psychol.,* 142(1938), 67–134.
[17] *Ibid.,* p. 128.   [18] *Ibid.,* p. 130.

enced by the special peculiarities of the schematic figures employed.

In everyday life when we experience the face of another person as the form under which traits of his personality manifest themselves, it is not only the structure or architecture of the face but also what Philip Lersch calls "the expressive traces" [19] which determine what stamp we experience. The way in which the face has been furrowed, or in other ways marked, by the frequently recurring facial expressions, often creates a special pattern which becomes a part of the experienced stamp, as when we experience another as friendly, worried, tensed up, suspicious, open, determined, etc. Stamps of this kind are often experienced as the forms under which more lasting traits or attitudes manifest themselves, as distinct from the corresponding expressions where the mental aspect is a specific momentary condition or attitude.

Not only the face but the whole body build may influence the experienced stamp; it is generally accepted, and certainly by the adherents of Kretschmer's theories, that the corpulent individual is perceived as more of an extrovert, the lean as more of an introvert. Further, the way the body is held plays an important role; the depressed, "low" carriage or the strutting carriage is immediately perceived as a stamp by most people. It is possible to describe a man as "stiff-necked," admire his "straight personality" and feel sorry for the person who has been "bent by adversity."

There are many other bodily conditions which may influence the way in which a person's inner life will manifest itself to us. If we note the bodily characteristics which people in general—more or less seriously—include when they perceive the character of others as inherent in their outward appearance, we shall gather a rather astonishing collection: the structure and distribution of the hair; the color, size, and shape of the eyes; the size and shape of the ears, nose, mouth, hands, and nails; the length of arms and legs; the size and position of the feet, etc. Mostly the experience of a connection between outer traits and mental aspects is extremely vague, and the person having the experience will often repudiate

[19] Philipp Lersch, *Gesicht und Seele* (Munich, 1932), p. 22.

them if he is forced to formulate them explicitly. Nevertheless, in some cases they do play a not insignificant role in contributing to the undifferentiated impression of the personality of another, an impression which often remains the only aspect with which we deal, as in the case of people whom we meet only once or with whom we never have anything but superficial contact.

In a more special way it is also true that different theories about the connection between bodily and psychological characteristics will provide their adherents with the possibility of perceiving some very special kinds of "stamps"; they can be given in a more immediate way, depending on how familiar the observer is with the theory in question, and how much experience he has in applying them. For the adherent of chiromancy the lines of the hand become the form under which the person's mental aspects (and his fate) manifest themselves, and a phrenologist could perceive the character of the person by observing the shape of the skull.

There is yet another area to be mentioned, that of clothes. The dress of a person not only tells us something about the sex of that person, and often his occupation, nationality, and social position, as Flügel says;[20] it may also form a part of the stamp and to some extent determines which mental aspects we shall perceive as his. In many cases the dress will play a very important role in the immediate first impression we gain of another person. The clothes, and in particular the way in which they are worn, are included in our perception when we perceive the personality of others as intrinsic to their outward appearance.[21]

We have mentioned dress here because in most cases we perceive it as belonging immediately to the appearance of another person; but if we interest ourselves in the specific dress as a consequence partly of the way in which the clothes have been chosen, when they were first bought, and partly of "dressing behavior" on that particular morning, then we are dealing with another kind of

[20] J. C. Flügel, *The Psychology of Clothes* (London, 1930), p. 15.

[21] Attempts have been made to establish the study of dress as a branch of the study of personality in analogy with graphology. See Marga Braganz-Lehmann, "Kleid und Persönlichkeit," *Industrielle Psychotechnik,* 12 (1935), 238–48.

psychoid entity belonging to the next group, that of behavior results.

We shall now proceed a little further with psychic aspects of the "stamp," the mental traits which may be intrinsic to the perception of the behavior and the total external appearance of our fellow men. We may be dealing with relatively simple and relatively well defined traits: thus we may experience the man as friendly or depressed or pessimistic or pedantic or arrogant. Or there may be several characteristics at the same time; in this case they may manifest themselves relatively independently of each other, but often they will influence and modify each other in our experience of the personality of the man, so that the total impression we receive becomes rather complicated and difficult to analyze into individual characteristics.

In an interesting investigation Asch [22] demonstrated how different perceived mental traits can influence each other when they are presented verbally. He conducted the following experiment: Two groups of experimental subjects, A and B, were presented with a list of character traits of an imaginary person and instructed to form a general impression of the person and then to characterize him in a few sentences. In one experimental series, Group A was given the following list of words: intelligent, skillful, industrious, warm, determined, practical, cautious. And Group B was given the same list, with the one difference that "warm" had been replaced by "cold." We shall give an example of the kind of descriptions which the groups produced: A: "A scientist performing experiments and persevering after many setbacks. He is driven by the desire to accomplish something that would be of benefit." And from Group B: "A rather snobbish person who feels that his success and intelligence set him apart from the run-of-the-mill individual. Calculating and unsympathetic." [23]

[22] S. E. Asch, "Forming Impressions of Personality," *J. Abn. and Soc. Psychol.*, 41 (1946), 258–90.
[23] *Ibid.*, p. 263.

Another series of his experiments demonstrates the importance of the order in which the traits are presented to the subjects. For example, Group A was given the following list: intelligent, industrious, impulsive, critical, stubborn, envious. Group B was given the same list but in the reverse order: envious, stubborn, critical, impulsive, industrious, intelligent. One description from Group A reads: "Is a forceful person, has his own convictions and is usually right about things. Is self-centered and desires his own way." And a description from Group B: "This person's good qualities such as industry and intelligence, are bound to be restricted by jealousy and stubbornness. The person is emotional. He is unsuccessful because he is weak and allows his bad points to cover up his good ones." [24]

These experiments, together with many others, demonstrate that the experimental subjects perceive the person described as a totality; the traits listed were organized within this totality and they modify each other in a way which is dependent, among other things, on the traits surrounding each one of them and on the order of presentation. For example, Asch finds that certain traits become more central in the perceived personality and become the determinants of the way in which certain other, more dependent, traits are included in the totality. A change of a single trait may change not only this single aspect of the experienced whole but also many other aspects—at times all aspects of the whole.

Of course, it is not possible to transfer Asch's results directly to the problems with which we are dealing: perception of the character of a real, concrete person—something stressed by Asch himself. [25] Everything becomes more involved because we are not presented with the characteristics of a person but have to discover them for ourselves.

When we are dealing with real people, the traits which manifest themselves in our experience are very often not at all clear and simple characteristics, as already discussed above. The mental as-

[24] *Ibid.,* p. 270.   [25] *Ibid.,* pp. 288 ff.

pect of the perceived stamp may be a complex one for various reasons and in different ways. Here we may mention the curious "ambivalence" which is generated in a rather straightforward and direct way in our perception of another person when we realize that he is attempting to appear different from what he is—so that, for example, we get the impression that he is trying to hide his self-assertion under a self-deprecating appearance, or his insecurity under a swagger. But this experience that it is possible, as it were, to see through the "outer layers" of the personality and get hold of something "deeper" is not limited to cases where it seems to us that the person is more or less consciously trying to act differently. Very often we experience in a direct fashion that "he is not really as stupid as he acts" or "she is not as aggressive as she appears to be," and so on. In these cases some of the experienced "stamp" manifests itself with an air of belonging to the "surface" of the personality and has nothing to do with the deeper layers.

There are certain differences between the first impression, the way in which we perceive a person's character the first time we encounter him, and the way in which we perceive the person later when we are dealing with him, meet him in different situations, "get to know him." Sometimes it turns out that the first impression does not correspond at all to the way in which we perceive the man when we have come to know him better; in other cases the two "percepts" may correspond to a greater or smaller degree.

Lehtovaara [26] has attempted to investigate "the reliability" of short limited first impressions related to certain traits in the observed persons by comparing the judgments made on the basis of first impressions with information about the individual in question produced from other sources (character descriptions given by teachers and schoolmates, academic record, psychological investigations, etc.). He found that such first impressions vary considerably for individual observers but that, overall, they contain judgments which

[26] Arvo Lehtovaara, "First Impressions," *Studia Psychologica et Paedagogica,* 2 (1948), pp. 121–52.

accord with the information gathered from other sources; also there is a considerably higher correlation between the descriptions obtained by the two methods than could be obtained by pure chance.

Lehtovaara instructed the persons to be rated to move about and for one minute to conduct a conversation with the experimenter. In an investigation by Cleeton and Knight [27] thirty individuals were rated with regard to a number of characteristics while they were sitting on a stage, ten at a time. There were seventy judges who were accustomed to estimating people for the purpose of employment and their judgments correlate to a considerable extent. Divided into the same groups of ten, the subjects were then rated by twenty persons who met them daily and knew them well, and also in this case there was a good mutual agreement. The correlations between the judgments made by close friends and by "casual observers" show a general positive tendency, but it is not of such a magnitude, concluded the authors, that they can be considered significant.[28]

In our daily perception of the character of others, interest is not limited to a few well-defined traits; we are dealing instead with a more or less clearly defined total impression. Under these circumstances we almost always find that there is a great difference between the way in which we perceive a person's personality at the beginning of our acquaintanceship and the way in which we perceive him later on when we have gained a closer knowledge of him. Among other things, the impression almost always becomes much more differentiated; frequently it also becomes much more definite in general structure. We often find that as long as we do not know another person very well there is an aura of something temporary and intermediate around our experience of his personality; but later, as our knowledge is deepened, our experience of him appears as something much more definite and certain.

[27] Glen Cleeton and F. B. Knight, "Validity of Character Judgments Based on External Criteria," *J. Applied Psychol.,* 8 (1924), 215–31.
[28] *Ibid.,* p. 229.

At the same time it often happens that the stamp becomes the form under which more deep-seated traits of the personality manifest themselves; the purely external parts of behavior and appearance play a minor role and more central factors are immediately apparent. If we do know another person very well, we may perceive the deeper traits in him, whether he is ill or well, angry or happy, sleepy or alert. More incidental changes on the surface of things no longer hide the inner factors, as they so often do in the case of persons whom we do not know well.

Another side of this problem is connected with the way in which behavior is controlled by custom and habit or other similar systems of rules; if we do not know the rules which determine the behavior of others, it is often difficult to perceive the behavior pattern as a personal stamp. The individual character of an officer may be rather well hidden under the military bearing, in the eyes of a person who does not know much about soldiers; that of a clergyman under the clerical. But for the person who acquires a more intimate knowledge of the military or clerical estate it will often be possible to perceive the man "through" the behavior pattern established by his belonging to the particular estate or class. If we see much of medical men, we do not perceive a physician as a physician only. We perceive that he is a doctor in a certain well-defined way; thus his way of being a doctor may become the form under which his personality manifests itself together with many of its special peculiarities.

If we see a person often, it will frequently happen that as time goes by we perceive him differently from the way in which we perceive him at first. We can describe an important aspect of this change by saying that different details in the perceived stamp are becoming a part of the total pattern. Often the result of this change is that a given physical stimulus does not correspond to the same experience as it did to begin with. The face which appeared unintelligent to us may very well appear intelligent as we experience how wise the man is, and in the end it may be very difficult to experience any part of his facial expression as stupid. If we do succeed in perceiving it as partly stupid or unintelligent, this particular part will then be perceived as something belonging to the surface only and no longer will it be perceived as being the form under which his intelligence manifests itself. It is a mask only. Behavior which at one time we found brusque and uninviting may lose this quality completely and be experienced as friendly when we have gained a knowledge of the man and his friendly attitude.

When details in the experienced stamp become in this way a part of a much wider pattern, it frequently happens that not only the mental aspect of the psychoid entity is changed but also the material aspect: we are dealing with a completely new experienced entity. A face not only "means" something else, it also *looks* quite different.

Things which we noticed in the beginning of the friendship may disappear completely into the background if they do not play any role for the more comprehensive pattern which we are now experiencing, so that we are barely able to experience these details any more. Time and again it happens that details which in the beginning were outstanding, and even dominated the experience of the other person with regard to his appearance, voice, gestures, dress or behavior, retreat so far into the background that we are quite surprised when people meet the person for the first time and remark on these aspects. It may happen that the perceived stamp in a way becomes independent of the external aspects of the person; our perception of his character may to a large extent become independent of the details of his appearance and behavior. Step by step the details which at one time dominated the perceived stamp will change and be replaced by other psychoid entities where it is the perception of the person's deep-seated traits which will determine our experience of the external aspects, perhaps gathered together in a more comprehensive pattern. Two things will then happen: Certain traits which are of no importance to the new totality will nearly disappear from the experience while others, which until now were nearly neglected, may come to the fore and gain real importance.

The formation of the more comprehensive pattern takes place when we gain the kind of experiences with regard to the person which will permit us to perceive his actual behavior as forms under which extended patterns appear—in such a way that we experience his behavior as directed toward certain more distant objects and guided by more or less permanent attitudes or intentions.

Then we may experience the behavior of another person as "personality reactions," as Kaila[29] calls them, which we are to interpret as reactions which carry a stamp of great inclusiveness, corresponding to a very comprehensive "life-field . . . where the personality makes full use of earlier experiences and considers the consequences of his actions, while at the same time setting up his goals and ideals which makes it possible to resist immediate impulses."[30]

When we have reached a perception of the character of another person in the form of such a comprehensive "behavior-pattern," it may have a very important influence on the way in which we experience his individual actions. The same behavior sequence, carried out by two different persons, may not cause the same experienced behavior. A young lady has told me the following observation, which is a nice example of how strongly the experienced behavior can be shaped according to the pattern to which it belongs. The young lady saw Professor X, whom she dislikes, walk on the pavement in front of her and in the same direction as she was walking, and she thought: "This man does walk in a very theatrical and pompous fashion; he clearly thinks very highly of himself." When she got a little closer to the man, she saw that it was not at all Professor X but her beloved teacher, Doctor Y, whom she thought was not rated according to his deserts because of his

[29] Eino Kaila, *Personlighedens psykologi* (*Psychology of Personality*) (Copenhagen, 1948), pp. 279 ff.
[30] *Ibid.*, p. 280.

humility. And now, walking just behind Dr. Y., she thought: "This man's whole appearance shows his humility; his walk is so straightforward and humble." Only then did she realize the curious fact that the same person had made two such different impressions on her. The story illustrates clearly the way in which our perception of another person decides how we perceive his individual actions as a stamp.

The stamp is of great importance when we consider how we perceive the behavior of others and not least their actions. Therefore I have described it in relatively great detail, but there will be many opportunities to deal with a whole series of problems connected with the experienced "stamp" a little later when we discuss how we experience the behavior of others.

2. *Behavior Traces*

The second main group of the psychoid entities we have called "behavior results" or "behavior traces." Many human behavioral events may appear to us in such a fashion that we have an immediate perception of them taking place at the present time. Furthermore, as described above, it will often happen that a shorter sequence becomes the form under which a more comprehensive sequence is manifested. But it is also true of many events that they are apparent to us after the event itself has taken place because of our perception of the "traces" which the process has left behind. The traces become the elements of yet another entity—the finished or completed event. It may be a passing trace, as quickly disappearing smoke after a fire, or it may be a lasting trace, as mountain ranges formed by geological disturbances. Such traces of weather or wind, animals or plants, function in various degrees as ways in which the events that have produced them manifest themselves. The topic of our present discussion is traces created by human activity.

Of course, not all results of human behavior constitute what we have called "psychoid entities." Traces can point to human activity without any mental aspect being intrinsic to our perception of the action or event. When we perceive the traces, it may happen that the behavior to which they point appears very indistinctly to us; in some cases there is not much more in our perception than the mere existence of human beings, as when in darkness, in a deserted and isolated place, we catch sight of a glimpse of light and immediately perceive that there must be people there. The appearance at a distance of a column of smoke or steam will often be the form under which not only the fire but also some human activity, perhaps not too well defined, manifests itself. That the entity "human activity" in such cases can appear rather immediately without any further consideration is something I have myself experienced on a journey in Iceland. Time and again, when at a distance I saw the steam column from hot springs, I caught myself in brief fleeting deliberations on the question whether it was a train or a factory or something else. These thoughts never became real speculations before I realized that in Iceland such columns of steam indicate a special phenomenon which has nothing to do with human activity.

If I walk along the seashore and see some footprints in the sand, I shall in most cases perceive quite immediately that a man has walked there, but rarely will I have the experience of some mental aspect of the person. In some cases, however, the traces may indicate a mental aspect or become the form under which a mental aspect of the person manifests itself to me. If they change course and lead up to an object lying on the shore, I may perceive that the man has intended to look closer at this object; if from the prints I can see that the man has been dancing and jumping along the shore, I may perceive him as having been very happy; and if I see footprints which show that the person has always walked around wet spots and always avoided stepping on them, I may perceive him as being of a careful and pedantic nature.

With regard to classification, it is possible to divide our perceptions of the results of human behavior as psychoid entities into the same groups that we used in the survey of the psychoid entities arising out of our direct perception of other people.

The traces may indicate the actions which produced them and be the form under which both the material sequence and the purpose manifest themselves; we shall then talk of "action traces" or "action results." Or the traces may indicate an emotion or some other mental condition which has dominated the person during the behavior sequence which produced the traces; we shall then talk about "expressive traces." Finally, the results of a behavior sequence may be the form under which mental aspects of the person manifest themselves, so that we perceive the traces as indicating or pointing to some aspects of the personality of the man; such entities we shall call "stamp traces." I shall now deal with each of these in turn.

ACTION TRACES

It is possible to perceive many of the events with which we deal in everyday life as being action traces. Tranekjær Rasmussen stresses "that included among the significant features of many events (e.g. objects fashioned or made by man, situations resulting from human action) is their indication that they are the result of actions." [31] Tranekjær Rasmussen divides the group I have called "action traces" into two groups.

One group is defined by the fact that creation of the object has been the goal of an action. This applies for example to objects such as manufactured tools or utensils, etc., to various situations such as the attainment of a bodily posture, an amorous conquest, or the like. The other group is characterized by saying that it is simply the by-product of an action, as for example footprints in the sand, an "intermediate" position on the way to a much desired social position, etc. We introduce the

[31] Tranekjær Rasmussen, "Undersøgelser over Erkendelsen."

expression "action product" as the name of such action results which cannot be regarded as goals.[32]

We are dealing directly with a psychoid entity when an object is perceived as the result of behavior in such a way that it appears as what Tranekjær Rasmussen has called an "action goal," something which the acting individual intended to create. This perception has both a material and a psychological aspect; the psychological aspect has to do with a mental quality outside ourselves.

With regard to the experience of "action products" it is characteristic that nothing in the perception suggests that the person had the intention to create or make them. But nevertheless such entities may often be properly called psychoid entities, because they more or less directly indicate the action by which they came into existence. The man sharpening his pencil does not intend to produce the wood shavings; he intends to sharpen the pencil. Nevertheless, the shavings may be the form under which the action in its two aspects manifests itself, so that the action goal may be intrinsic to the perception of the action product.

But frequently the question of whether an event will appear as action goal or action product will depend on the totality of the perceived situation: whether we perceive that a person has emptied his glass with only the intention of emptying the glass or instead as a consequence of quenching his thirst will depend on our total perception of the man in the particular situation.

Things created by human activity form a great part of all the events with which we deal in everyday life. We usually perceive such events as psychoid entities, as action traces. This does not mean, however, that we *always* perceive them in this way. Often a special attitude or set is necessary to perceive an object mainly as resulting from an action; the object may be defined by its utility, it is made for something, and it will often be this aspect which dominates in our experience. What Tranekjær Rasmussen has

[32] *Ibid.*

called the action product may often be more easily perceived as the form under which the relevant action giving rise to the product manifests itself; just because no "utility-determination" is given with it, it has no use, no independent "meaning."

But if we begin to take a deeper interest in the utility-determination of an object, it may result in its appearing as an action result. For example, if we cannot quite see what is the use of a particular object, then we speculate on what the maker really had in mind; or we may regard an object as imperfectly suited for its purpose and adopt a critical attitude to the goal we perceive the maker as having set for himself. Or it could be the reverse: we find an object to be exceptionally well made and admire the good idea of the man who produced it.

Objects of this kind—tools and other things for everyday use— may often appear as action traces in a very complicated way. If an object, appearing as an action result, has been produced by industrial mass production, I will frequently perceive not only the form under which the action of the worker manifests itself but also, and more likely, the action of the inventor, technician, or artist who has given the object its particular form; and I may also perceive that the object as a whole has been made not by a single workman only but by a great number of workers, as for example with a motor car or a pencil.

When I perceive a certain object to be an action result, it may be with reference to different actions. It may in a more general way refer to several actions at the same time, or it may in my personal perception become the form under which one single definite action manifests itself. If, for example, I sit and look at my fountain pen, I may perceive it with reference to the action of the inventor who constructed the first fountain pen, or to the shaping of this particular model and to the man who designed it —or I may perceive it as the result of the action of the worker, or several workers, in the fountain pen factory. The same object, perceived as action trace, may then refer to different actions each with its own goal, carried out by different persons, depending on my attitude and intention at the moment of my perception.

Objects of this kind constitute only one group in a large total number of perceived action results. Every day we deal with many different events, where certain perceived situations, structures, and arrangements may appear to us as "action traces." Often an action has resulted in certain changes in the perceived surroundings, so that these changes may be perceived as results of the action, as action goals or as action products.

In this way our daily life is full of "social contacts" in the form of psychoid entities, which always refer to the action of other people, even if we do not come into direct contact with these people. These entities may not immediately appear as action results; this may depend upon dominant needs, interests, and attitudes present in the immediate situation. Nor does everybody perceive such entities as action results to the same extent; there are wide individual differences, ranging from the person who perceives the people "behind the things" in almost every situation to the person who perceives only the things themselves, without any great interest in the social factors that have played a role in the origin of the objects.

But if we have the appropriate attitude, it is possible for many of us to perceive, for example, the food that is placed before us, or the position of the furniture in a room and the books on the shelves, or the hay in its stacks and the washing on the line, as action traces. Let me add that such traces in our perception of them may refer not only to the action in which they had their origin (in other words refer retroactively to an earlier behavior sequence); they may also refer proactively to the form under which a subsequent action manifests itself. A table already laid may refer to the action of laying it, which has been completed in the past, but it may also refer to the meal which is about to take place. When we see a taxi in front of the entrance, we may perceive the position of the car as the consequence of the action of the driver when he arrived, but more often it is likely to be experienced as directly referring to the departure of our guests, perhaps because we are more interested in this event.

In discussing the direct perception of the actions of others (see page 17 above), we explained how a perceived, brief behavior sequence may be the form under which a more comprehensive sequence manifests itself, so that the beginning of a sequence may be the form under which the whole sequence manifests itself. Actions of different kinds may be perceived as initial or introduction actions, perhaps as the first link of a pair or of a longer sequence. Insofar as an action trace is perceived as the result of just such an introductory action, it may also refer to a subsequent action or action sequence.

EXPRESSION TRACES

With regard to the other group of perceived results of behavior, the group that we have called "expression traces," it is characteristic that we are dealing here with behavior sequences that are not perceived as actions directed by a person's purpose or intention. Generally, such sequences do not leave behind any traces through which we can perceive the emotional state of the other person. There are, however, exceptions: a tear-stained handkerchief may become the form under which sorrow is manifested, and the trails left behind after an outbreak of rage may indicate the mental state of the person during the behavior sequence. Such traces we shall call "pure expression traces," as they do not appear as the result of purposive action.

Quite commonly an action trace perceived as the result of an action might appear as an expression trace: perhaps the action may be perceived as springing from an emotional state so that the result of the action may also become the form under which the emotion is manifested, as, for example, when a murder of passion is perceived as an expression of jealousy or a gift as an expression of gratitude. The action is then perceived as the form under which the mental state is manifested, and consequently it is possible for the action result also to be perceived as an expression trace.

When we described the perception of emotional expressions, we explained how the way in which an action is carried out may become the form under which a mental state in the acting person is manifested. In relation to this phenomenon, we may find that the action results indicate some aspects of the way in which the sequence develops and may provide a form under which we can detect the mental state dominating the person while the action was in progress. A letter begun several times may lead us to perceive some kind of insecurity in the writer. An ashtray full of half-smoked cigarettes may generate a perception of the nervousness of the smoker. In these two situations we are concerned with what Tranekjær Rasmussen has called action products, and not action goals. Frequently it will be precisely the action products which indicate the mental state of the person during the behavior in question. Even if we do perceive the action products as partial reasons for the behavior of the person carrying out the action, they do not appear as determinants of the behavior in quite the same way as does the action goal. We perceive them less as a consequence of the problem to which a solution is being sought and, therefore, as more open to the influence of the acting person's dominant mental state. This does not prevent action goals from being perceived as indicative of an emotion or another mental state dominant in the acting person; for example, a particularly beautiful table arrangement may be perceived as the expression of happiness because of a welcome visit.

STAMPED TRACES

Just as a perceived behavior sequence together with the goal-directedness that forms an integral part of it may be the form under which the character traits of the behaving person are manifested, so also the consequences of behavior may, in our perception, point to traits in the personality of the individual. And sometimes we find that it is specifically the action results that become significant in our perception of the way in which we experience the mental qualities of another person. As Adam Smith put it: "Though the intentions of any person should be ever so proper and beneficent, on the one hand, or ever so improper and malevolent, on the other, yet, if they fail in producing their effects, his merit seems imperfect in the one case, and his demerit incomplete in the other." [33] The consequences springing from an action influence greatly the way in which we regard the action. And we can add also that the way in which we perceive the mental aspects of a man will often depend very much on the way in which we experience not only his intentions and his actions but also the results springing from them. Adam Smith seems to discuss this aspect when he says:

Even the merit of talents and abilities which some accident has hindered from producing their effects, seems in some measure imperfect, even to those who are fully convinced of their capacity to produce them. The general who had been hindered by the envy of ministers from gaining some great advantage over the enemies of his country regrets the loss of opportunity forever after. Nor is it only upon account of the public he regrets it. He laments that he was hindered from performing an action which would have added a new lustre to his character in his own eyes, as well as in those of every other person.[34]

Both in his own eyes and in those of others, he is less imposing than he would have been if he had actually succeeded—even if the plans he had made were ever so good and would have had the hoped-for effect if they had been carried out.

In many cases our experience of the mental qualities of other people depends very much on the perception of behavioral consequences. It is not only with regard to false prophets that it is true to say: "By their fruits you shall know them." [35] In order for us to perceive a man as artistically gifted it is generally necessary that

[33] *The Theory of Moral Sentiments*, p. 199.   [34] *Ibid.*, pp. 202–3.
[35] Matthew 7:16.

we are able to see a work of his art as an expression of this artistic gift. It is generally true with regard to many traits, abilities, and skills that we evaluate them from the point of view of their overt products. And if we then assess the man to be a genius, we may perceive virtually everything from his hand as valuable, just because, for us, it appears to be an outward manifestation of his genius.

Sometimes the perception of a single behavioral consequence may be decisive for the way in which important traits in a person's character manifest themselves to us, especially when the relevant product deviates from what we perceive as the typical product. If a man has created one great work of art, we may regard him as a genius, even if he never produces anything of importance again. If a man has committed a crime, many will perceive his personality in terms of this one behavioral consequence. To many people, a murderer is a murderer and nothing else. They see in him only the abstract characteristic of being a murderer; and this single characteristic swallows up all the rest of his human nature, as Hegel says in his essay *Wer denkt abstrakt.*[36]

Examinations and other such tests can be regarded as methods that aim at eliciting behavioral products which can become the form under which more or less well defined mental traits in the examinee manifest themselves, such as intelligence, ability, potentialities, skills. The examination performance itself gives people with special training the possibility of observing these traits in the candidate. On the basis of this experience a judgment can be formed and the examiner may describe or assess the performance, quantitatively, so that the behavioral consequence is presented in a form whereby those who are unable to judge the examination performance themselves may experience the behavioral consequences as more or less direct forms through which the man's ability in one or more fields manifests itself.

[36] G. W. F. Hegel, *Werke,* vol. 17, Vollst. Ausgabe (Berlin, 1835), p. 403. (Who is thinking in the abstract).

A similar principle is used in many psychological tests. The subject to be investigated carries out various activities, the results of which become, for the psychologist, the form under which his traits may manifest themselves. On the basis of his observation of the mental attributes of the subject, the psychologist will work out a description which permits the traits in question to be available to others (who themselves have no possibility of experiencing the behavioral consequences directly, as the form under which the man's character trait or other qualities can be manifested).

We have seen that it is not only a man's intentions and actions which can become the form under which his mental characteristics manifest themselves but also the way in which the action is carried out. Similarly, it is also true that action traces may point to characteristics in the personality of the person carrying out the action, by showing something of the behavior pattern during the action sequence. A single action result may, for example, point to a pedantic or an unsystematic behavior pattern, to an impulsive or a deliberate one, and this aspect of the action trace may, by itself, be the form under which the trait manifests itself, if it points to a behavioral pattern as the form under which a mental aspect manifests itself.

Furthermore, our previous discussion of the behavior pattern as the form under which perceived mental aspects manifest themselves is also true in this case: the fact that a behavior pattern is perceived as characteristic of a person does not necessarily mean that it is experienced as a stamp. In the same way, we can quite easily perceive a behavioral consequence as characteristic of a person without at the same time experiencing it as indicating a trait in his personality. That I can see from a picture that it has been painted by Matisse, or hear from a piece of music that is has been composed by Haydn, does not necessarily mean that I perceive traits of the creator's personality as implicit in my experience of a behavioral product which is characteristic of him.

Gordon Allport stresses "style" as the most complete form for what he calls expressive behavior. It has to do with behavior as a whole, not only with special abilities. "Everybody has his special style and in this way we can recognize compositions by Chopin, paintings by van Gogh and pastry by Aunt Sally." "Style," says Allport, "represents the most complete form of expressive behavior. . . . It is apparent that style is one of the most embracing concepts with which psychology has to deal." [37] By and large we can agree with Allport in this. But it may be worthwhile to repeat that, in everyday perception of the behavioral products of others, the fact that the style is evident to us does not necessarily mean anything but a perception of its relationship to the person who produced them.

Of course, in many cases and for many people the style may appear as a stamp. It is probably true for most of us that certain experiences may result in the forging of a connection between the perception of such a personal style, as it appears in a behavioral consequence, and certain forms under which mental aspects of the person manifest themselves, so that the style thereafter may be given for us as a stamp.

In the study of handwriting, graphology, attempts have been made to find connections of this nature between, on the one hand, perceived style as it is provided in a certain kind of behavioral event and, on the other hand, certain observations of the person's mental traits. The goal has been to formulate methods that would make it possible from an observation of the person's handwriting to arrive at an assessment of his character traits and other mental characteristics. "One would expect," states the Danish graphologist Annelise Garde, "that hand-writing to a large extent expresses the mental structure of a person," and she assumes that the writer, as Max Pulver expresses it, creates his self-portrait through handwriting. The analysis of the strokes, i.e., "the development (in the photographic sense) of the picture," so that it becomes visible to the ordinary, non-graphologically trained eye, is done by determin-

[37] *Personality*, pp. 489–90.

ing a number of characteristics belonging to written symbols and by noting the meaning of these characteristics.[38]

According to Annelise Garde, if we wish to arrive at an assessment of the character traits of a writer by studying the strokes of his handwriting, the technique consists, among other things, in getting to know persons whose handwriting one has studied on previous occasions. There will then be an opportunity to make comparisons between graphological analysis and the results of direct observation.[39]

There is no doubt that an experienced graphologist on the basis of the strokes found in handwriting develops a fairly detailed and differentiated impression of the personality of the writer. The only problem is the degree of agreement between the graphologist's impressions of the man's mental characteristics, on the one hand, and the personality trait which we eventually experience through other channels, on the other. A thorough investigation of this relationship must be made before graphology can be seriously considered as a method to be employed in the study of personality. But as Tranekjær Rasmussen states in his preface to Annelise Garde's book: "As yet it has not been possible to conduct sufficiently exact investigations of a statistical nature of the connection between the strokes found in handwriting and the character of the writers, and this, among other reasons, for the very good reason that so far it has not been possible, with a sufficient degree of exactitude and objectivity, to determine particular character traits in a person or their degrees of strength."

The problem of how far one can rely on one's impressions of the mental characteristics of others—whatever this means—is not only a problem for graphology but is important for all attempts to unravel questions concerning character and personality. I think, however, that it is of importance for the solution of these problems

[38] Annelise Garde et al., *Grafologi i Grundtræk* (*Outline of Graphology*) (Copenhagen, 1946), p. 12.

[39] *Ibid.,* p. 13.

first to take an interest in the question of how we actually experience other people and their behavior, without the help of special methods. One of the purposes of this essay is to throw some light on this question.

3. Psychoid Entities in the Language

The experience of hearing or reading words and sentences has several aspects. In ordinary situations, we normally understand what we hear; words and sentences refer more or less directly to some object. Linguistic entities may be the form under which a great number of other entities in our experience manifest themselves, and in our daily life we deal with great numbers of entities which appear verbally before us. It is also true that a large number of the events which we experience are dealt with by us only in their verbal manifestations.

We can describe the reason why entities can manifest themselves for us in this way by saying that for one who has learned the language the words represent certain entities; with Jørgen Jørgensen we can say that they have a representative or semantic function.[40] In this connection Carnap has stated that there exists a "sign-relationship" (*Zeichenbeziehung*) between physical entities, which "mean something, and that which they 'mean', e.g., between the written letters 'Rome' and the city of Rome." [41]

In modern linguistics, founded by F. de Saussure and continued by many others, among them Louis Hjelmslev, there is a different way of describing the reason why entities can appear in verbal form. Hjelmslev does not regard the sign as an expression referring to a content outside the sign itself; the sign is a totality which consists of a connection between an expression and a content, and he uses the word "sign" as the name for the compound unit of con-

---

[40] Jørgen Jørgensen, *Psykologi paa biologisk grundlag* (*Psychology on a Biological Foundation*) (Copenhagen, 1941–46), p. 455.
[41] Rudolf Carnap, *Der logische Aufbau der Welt* (Berlin, 1928), p. 19.

tent and of expression, established by the solidarity that he calls the "signfunction." [42]

But let us limit ourselves to language as we deal with it when entities manifest themselves verbally. If we are familiar with the language in question, then it is true that, more often than not, we experience the entities intrinsic to the perceived words and sentences. They may appear very directly so that in a sense we seem to be dealing with the thing itself through its verbal manifestation. Normally there is no sense of dichotomy in the perception, no experience of a verbal entity plus the entity to which it refers.

PSYCHOID ENTITIES WHERE THE MENTAL ASPECT IS PROVIDED SEMANTICALLY

Among all the entities that may be provided verbally, we shall first consider cases where words and sentences represent something mental in other people. Here we are dealing with a special form of psychoid entity where the material aspect consists of sounds or written signs. The mental aspect manifests itself more or less directly with the material aspect. The mental aspect includes all psychological entities that can be described or indicated by linguistic means. These may appear to us when another person is speaking about some personal mental state or when a third person says something concerning the mental states of another. Both of these representations are of great importance in our daily interactions with other people and in our total perception of other people and their behavior. Generally, however, the greatest importance attaches to an individual's remarks about his own psychological states. In most situations where we are dealing with people, these psychoid entities will influence our perception of others and they often enter into our perception of their actions, feelings, and character traits in a decisive manner. For example, we may see that a man is preparing to leave and we may hear him say:

[42] Louis Hjelmslev, *Omkring sprogteoriens grundlæggelse* (Copenhagen, 1943), pp. 44 ff.

"I'd better get home." We see that a man is hesitating and hear him say: "I am not too sure . . ." Or we perceive that an old lady is very charming and hear someone who perhaps knows her well say: "Isn't she a lovely and charming person?"

In the case of many mental entities, such as thoughts, considerations, and opinions, it is generally true that we perceive them via verbal representations and that a more differentiated and accurate experience of them is possible only when they do manifest themselves verbally. In certain situations we can "see what the man intends to do," but if we want a more precise or explicit experience of it we shall have to ask him about it.

When such psychoid entities are represented verbally, they may often appear rather directly. The man's thoughts and opinions may manifest themselves through the words he speaks. In certain cases the perception of the mental aspect may be less direct; it may even happen that the words may be perceived as referring to something mental but that the entity represented manifests itself only in a rather vague manner. This case is of particular interest to us when we are dealing with psychoid verbal entities, even though it is not specific to this but is a phenomenon that may appear in all perception of language.

A very vague reference may be perceived if we are not too familiar with the language which is being used. Under such circumstances we may perceive that words and sentences refer to something rather indefinite, or we may feel rather uncertain with regard to the meaning that we perceive. We almost always perceive a certain degree of reference, provided we actually perceive the sounds or the written characters as language. And even in some instances where we do not know the language at all, and where the words therefore do not represent definite entities, we may still have a definite perception of their meaning "something," although we do not know what it is. Later, we shall see that something analogous may be of great importance when we observe the behavior of other people. Here we shall take the opportunity to investigate a little further the problem within the area of linguistic understanding.

A reading of the following sentences will probably give most people the feeling that they have not understood anything of it: *Nin porth zadilkin al muchathin milko prim al elmin enthoth dal heben ensouim. Jifat gudik pledof vadelo ko jison smalik oka.* In the reader's perception of them these words probably do not refer to any very definite entities. Yet for many people there will be a certain vague reference to something, an experience that the words do mean something or other, though we do not know what it is. If we spend a little time on these strange sentences, it may be that some of the words will appear more clearly in perception and others continue to be rather vague; indefinite and rather temporary meanings may appear. If I now mention that the first sentence is taken from Rabelais' *Gargantua et Pantagruel,* second book, Chapter 9, where Panurge addresses Pantagruel and his comrades in thirteen different tongues, among them several meaningless homemade ones, and that the sentence quoted is derived from such a language specimen, then the earlier perception that the words mean something would probably disappear completely or perhaps be replaced by the perception that they only look as if they had a meaning.

But the second of the two sentences does have a meaning. It is a sentence in the artificial language called Volapük, and most of the works used here have been made by changing and abbreviating English words. *Jifat* means "mother": *ji* (from "she") is used as a prefix indicating the feminine gender and *fat* means "father"; *gudik* means "good" with the suffix *ik* indicating an adjective; *pledof* means "play," with the suffix *of* indicating the person; *vadelo* means "every day" (*del* from "day"); *ko* means "with"; *jison* means "daughter"; *smalik* means "small"; *oka* means "her." *Jifat gudik pledof vadelo ko jison smalik oka* therefore means: "The good mother plays every day with her small daughter." In most cases the words will now not only mean something but something very definite; and even if the entities represented are not provided directly, nevertheless they will appear relatively clearly. The perception may have changed its character completely when it is compared with what was present when the sentence was read the first time.

VERBAL EXPRESSIONS EXPERIENCED AS INFORMATION

The problems that arise when we do not understand words or sentences may resemble the conditions under which we encounter objects, tools, machines, or instruments the use of which we do not know. We perceive that they have a use but a more detailed definition of their purpose is not available to us. Under certain circumstances such a perception may result in the object acquiring a special interest. We may feel a kind of obligation to discover its use, and may also, in this case, rely on the context in which the thing appears or on similarities with things we know. But if we try to solve this problem, we will often come to a point where the thing appears mainly as a result of an action, because we speculate on what the originator has intended to do with it. (See above page 41.) Something similar may happen when we are concerned with verbal expressions that we do not understand—and under certain conditions this may result in our becoming interested in what the man means to say. As a result of this interest the entity which appears in verbal form may acquire a definite quality of having a meaning and reality for the speaker—something which is present in his experience; as long as we do not understand the words, it is of course true that we do not know what his experience is, but we assume that something is present in his experience and this is the starting point when we attempt to understand what he says. This aspect of language experience may appear very clearly when comprehension causes difficulties, but for most people it may appear more or less distinctly as soon as the appropriate attitude or set is adopted. We are saying here that words and sentences are experienced as information when the entities represented appear to us in such a way that we perceive them in the way that they also appear to the speaker.

When verbal expressions are perceived in this way, i.e., as information, we are dealing with psychoid entities, for the psychological aspect of a perceived message is related to a mental state in the person who is communicating. If we adopt the appropriate set, it is generally possible for us to perceive something that is spoken or written as information, because we would be interested in this particular aspect of the experience, but ordinarily, when we listen or read, this is not the case. Often it is only the semantic aspect which appears perceptually. I may hear a man say: "The train is coming now," and perceive only the arrival of the train. The nature of the percept is similar to the percept that would arise if I myself had heard the sound of the coming train; only the form of the stimulus is different. The perception does not need to include any recognition that the entity is also apparent to the speaker—even though a different set would rapidly direct perception that way. Probably it is always possible to perceive a verbal utterance as information—in special situations, not to be discussed in detail here, but in the form of a perception that the phenomenal event present to the speaker is different from that which would be represented by the words he says, i.e., when we perceive that he does not speak the truth, does not say what he really thinks, etc. In rare cases we may perceive that a person does not realize what he is saying but wanted to say something else—and perhaps that he himself perceives that he is saying something different from what he intended.

If we are concerned not with what we hear but with what we read, the semantic aspect of the experience will often be the dominant aspect; we can read about something without taking any interest in the person who wrote it and without establishing any connection between the reading matter and an empathetic experience of it as having reality in the experience of the person who wrote it. For example, if I open an English–Danish Dictionary and see that "Queen" means "Dronning" in Danish, or if I see in the telephone directory the number of John Doe, then a very special set is needed in order to be aware of these things in terms of their having once been in the minds of the "authors." At other times, in the case of certain literary descriptions, for example, it may be that the reading material has a highly "informational" character and we may perceive the description predominantly, with an awareness of the perceptions of the author when he wrote it.

As I said, the experience of an utterance as appearing in the mind of the speaker will depend frequently upon a special set or attitude; informational aspects will often be less prominent. There are, however, certain utterances which are normally experienced as informational; this is the case where the semantic content of words represents something psychological about the speaker himself. We will experience this rather directly as something which is phenomenally present for the speaker when he says it.

In this case we experience that his own psychological state appears to a person in a special way. When A says: "I am happy today," and when B says: "A is glad today," then our experience of the words in the two cases may have the same semantic content. It is the same entity appearing under two different forms. If we focus upon the experience as information, then we find that this aspect is different in the two cases; we perceive that the way in which the event appears to B is different from the way in which it appears to A himself. It is also the case that when it is A himself who speaks of his own happiness we experience it as information, while this is not necessarily so when B speaks about A's happiness.

LANGUAGE EXPERIENCED AS BEHAVIOR

In the previous section we have discussed two kinds of psychoid entities: first, the experience that the semantic content of an expression represents some psychological state in the other person; next, the experience that what is said appears as such to the speaker, what we have called experienced information. These two kinds of psychoid entities are to be found only in language, and we do not find them in the perception of nonverbal behavior.

But in addition to these two special types, we may, in our experience of verbal material, be dealing with other kinds of psychoid entities with which we are familiar in relation to nonverbal behavior. Language may in some ways be experienced as a particular kind of behavior pattern, and may, as experienced behavior, become the form under which some psychological characteristics of others appear to us, just as with nonverbal forms of behavior.

It is possible therefore for a verbal expression to be experienced as an action in the same way that other behavior sequences may appear as actions. Just as a person's intentions may be perceived as integral to a behavior sequence (as described earlier in this work), an intention may also be manifested by a verbal expression. When we hear a man speak (or see him write), we may be interested in the question: "What is he doing?" and we may perceive him simply as "saying something" or "writing something." If we adopt the appropriate set, it may be immediately apparent to us that he intends to say what he says; in this respect language is no different from other behavior patterns. But, on the other hand, when we perceive what he is saying, we are dealing with the semantic aspect of the expression. If we now expand the perceptual situation in such a way that we take an interest in why he says it, then the utterance may be experienced in the same way as other nonverbal behavior patterns, i.e., as being a part of a more comprehensive sequence. The intentions of the speaker may be perceived as a part of this sequence. Just as the act of striking a match, for example, may be perceived as being a part of several other more comprehensive behavior sequences, so it may be possible for a given verbal utterance together with its perceived semantic content to become a part of one and then another behavior sequence. As a result of the particular characteristic that verbal utterances may be perceived both as actions and as parts of more comprehensive behavior sequences, a particular sentence with its semantic content may become the form under which quite different perceived intentions in the speaker manifest themselves, depending upon the behavior sequence of which it becomes a part.

In other, special cases the semantic content of the utterance may represent the intention or purpose of the speaker. The housewife says: "I should like you to come and eat now"; and we experience her intention as inherent semantically in the utterance. We may, however, perceive the same intention even if what she says has quite a different semantic content, as when she says: "The food is on the table." The semantic aspect of the two experiences is quite different but the experienced intention or purpose is identical. We could here mention in passing that in ordinary conversation with other people it may be less polite in some situations to declare one's intentions or wishes directly; among the various acceptable circumlocutions we find, for example, that of making one's intention known through a sentence, the semantic content of which does not say anything about the intention. The guest who wishes to leave does not say: "I want to go now," but perhaps: "It is rather late." Yet the host may perceive his intention just as directly in the latter case as he would have done in the former.

The intention which we will perceive in a speaker is therefore only partially dependent on what is semantically inherent in the words and sentences. It also depends on the total behavior sequence in which the words enter as partial sequences concomitant with nonverbal behavior patterns. This is true in many situations in daily life in which we perceive the actions of others.

The difference between experiencing utterances semantically or as actions may be particularly explicit when we are not certain what the speaker intends to communicate with his statements. We fully understand what he is saying, but we cannot understand why he says it, what his intentions are. The converse, that of not understanding what he says but clearly enough why he says it, is uncommon, but may occur. In the chapter cited above from *Gargantua and Pantagruel,* Rabelais lets Pantagruel answer Panurge, who has already expressed himself in eight different (and for the listeners incomprehensible) languages: "By Jove, my friend, I have no doubt that you are able to speak many languages, but do tell us in a language we understand what you wish to say." Pantagruel has not understood one word of all that Panurge has said, but he has perceived clearly enough that it is the intention of the latter to demonstrate that he knows a great number of languages.

Verbal utterances may also be perceived as expression in the same way that nonverbal behavior is. Then we are dealing with a psychoid entity where the material aspect is the word, which we hear or read, and the mental aspect is an emotion or some other mental condition in the speaker. Corresponding to expressive movements (facial expressions, movements of hands, etc.; see above page 19), we find in the linguistic area exclamations through which we can directly perceive not an intention but an emotional condition intrinsic to the words. If we hear somebody say: "Ah" or "Oh," we may perceive the emotion as intrinsic to the sound. Just as we do not perceive expressive movements as directed by an intention or purpose, so in this case we do not feel that the person planned to make the exclamation—unless we have the impression that he had the express intention of showing his feelings; in such a situation, of course, exclamations are frequently employed.

Corresponding to the way in which behavior patterns become the form through which feelings and other mental conditions in the acting person reveal themselves, we may perceive his style of speech, the tone of his voice, and so on, as the form under which such entities are manifested.

In this connection we may note that in special cases verbal utterances, perceived as expressions, and their semantic content may be symptomatic of the same psychological condition, i.e., when the utterances refer to this condition. If a person says in a shaky voice: "How nervous I am!" then his nervousness appears both as expressive behavior and in the semantic content. But apart from this special circumstance, the verbal behavior of a person, irrespective of what he says, will often be perceived as evidence of his feelings. Carnap talks about a relation of expression (*Ausdrucksbeziehung*) that exists between different movements, on the one hand, and the mental processes which they "express," on the other. In this connection he stresses that, in the case of language, it is necessary to distinguish between the relation of expression and the relation of sign in those instances where the same physical objects (the words as sound waves) stand at one and the same time in an expressive relation and a sign relation to the mental aspect. He thinks that spoken words always express something psychological regardless of their semantic content. By the tone of voice, the tempo or rhythm, and also by the choice of each word, together with the style, the words reveal something about the mental condition of the speaker.[43]

Even if verbal utterances are not always perceived as expressive, they do perform an important role in this connection and may, in many situations, be important as an essential form under which the emotional states of other people manifest themselves. Just as it was true for nonverbal behavior (see page 24 above), so it is true for language that the way in which it is spoken, indeed the way in which the language is being used, may be perceived as the manifestation of some more lasting psychological qualities of the speaker. In other words, verbal behavior may be experienced as what we have called a "stamp." Such traits as deliberateness, liveliness, trustworthiness, and kindness may appear inseparable from the way in which we perceive the person's speech and total use of language. We have already mentioned experiments using the radio, in which descriptions of persons were obtained on the basis of their voices alone.

In this respect also we may expect to find instances where the semantic aspect of the perception and its behavioral aspect become forms under which the same psychological quality appears. Thus a person may declare: "I am very deliberate," and his way of speaking at that moment be perceived as an example of the way in which this very quality manifests itself. Such cases appear to be less common in connection with the perception of a "stamp" than in con-

[43] *Der logische Aufbau der Welt*, pp. 24–25.

nection with the perception of expressive behavior. This may be due to the fact that, in the case of mental qualities in general, we do not perceive that they are consciously present for the man himself in the same way as they are evident to others; it may indeed be the case that we perceive that they are *not* evident to him in that way. We generally perceive that a girl does not perceive herself to be charming nor the child regard himself as "sweet"; if they do, our perception of them changes. Some kinds of psychological attributes may first appear in an observer's perception of the person; "Qualities such as 'brave' and 'proud' may depend to such an extent on the observer that the person to whom they are ascribed rightly denies them," as Rubin remarked.[44]

Let me conclude by recapitulating: In our experiences of the verbal behavior patterns emitted by others, the psychological aspects of another person may appear in several ways:

1. Psychological aspects may manifest themselves semantically, i.e., when the words spoken represent mental entities in the other person.

2. We may perceive that the semantic content that is evident to us is simultaneously consciously present for the speaker himself; this is what we call the perception of information.

3. Finally we may perceive language as a type of behavior and then it is possible that intentions, mental conditions, and more permanent psychological attributes of the speaker may be evident to us in the same way as in the experience of nonverbal behavior.

4. Psychoid Entities, Where the Psychic Aspect Is Not Concerned with Anything Mental in a Person

In this last group we shall discuss briefly a number of different psychoid entities which have in common the attribute that psy-

[44] E. Rubin, "Bemerkungen über unser Wissen von anderen Menschen," *Experimenta Psychologica* (Copenhagen, 1949), p. 33.

chological aspects perceived inherently with material aspects do not appear as having any connection with human mental life.

In general, when we observe the behavior of animals, it may appear to us as similar to human behavior. We perceive action directed by intention; we perceive expressive behavior where feelings and other mental conditions are evidenced immediately before us; and we may perceive psychological qualities such as wisdom, treachery, good-humoredness, wickedness, obstructionism, and obedience in approximately the same way that we experience it when we are dealing with our fellow humans. Often the perception of mental states in animals is less differentiated, and the psychological "traits" that present themselves to us may be rather simple and uncomplicated. Sometimes it may happen, however, that we deal with psychoid entities where the mental life of the animal is manifested as something quite complicated.

Which psychoid entities we experience in connection with animals depends partly on what the animal is doing but partly, and to a large extent, on our own attitude. Generally, with regard to animals we can perceive psychoid entities corresponding to those that we perceive as intrinsic to nonverbal behavior in human beings, i.e., action, expression, and stamp. As we have seen, language may be perceived not only with a semantic aspect but also as behavior, and it is not surprising, therefore, that we can perceive "verbal utterances" in animals where their behavior involves the production of sounds of a kind more or less similar to the sounds of human language.

Many people have had the experience of hearing animals speak not only their own language but also that of humans. Many have encountered parrots that speak and answer just as reasonably as any man. The English statesman William Temple tells us how Prince Maurice of Nassau in his day conducted extensive conversations with a clever Brazilian parrot with the help of two interpreters.[45] Darwin maintained that monkeys understand much of

[45] "and I had a Mind to know from his own Mouth, the Account of a common, but much credited story, that I had heard so often from many others, of an old

what is said to them by man,[46] and Leibniz told of a dog that could say more than thirty words with clear pronunciation and even give its master appropriate answers (*répondant même assez à propos à son maître*).[47] If one expects to find higher mental life in animals, then the limits for what one may experience are very wide. In his book on thinking horses, Karl Krall investigated the possibility of teaching horses to speak; they had learned to communicate by spelling words by stamping the foreleg according to a certain system. The horse, "Muhammed," was asked what one would have to do in order to speak; the horse spelled: *öfn munt* ("open mouth" —the horse used phonetic spelling!). Then they wrote on the blackboard: *warum du nigd munt öfn?* (Why don't you open the mouth?), and the horse answered: *weil kan nigd* ("because cannot"). They succeeded, however, in making him attempt to pronounce the sound "a," but the result was not very spectacular; the horse understood this himself, because one day he interrupted his talking exercises and, using the foreleg, spelled out: *ig hb kein gud sdim* (*ich habe keine gute Stimme;* I have no good voice).[48]

With regard to the question of feelings in animals, many people perceive rather clearly that animals feel in the same way as does man. Darwin stated: "The lower animals, like man, manifest pleasure and pain, happiness and misery. Happiness is never better exhibited than by young animals such as puppies, kittens, lambs, etc., when playing together like our own children. Even insects play

---

Parrot he had in Brasil, during his Government there, that spoke, and ask'd and answer'd common Questions like a reasonable Creature . . . I heard many Particulars of this Story, and assever'd by People hard to be discredit'd, which made me ask Prince Maurice what there was in it . . . I set down the words of this worthy Dialogue in French, just as Prince Maurice said them to me. I ask'd him, in what Language the Parrot spoke? and he said, In Brasilian. I ask'd Whether he understood Brasilian? He said, No; but he had taken Care to have two Interpreters by him, one a Dutch man that spoke Brasilian and t'other a Brasilian that spoke Dutch. That he ask'd them separately and privately, and both of them agreed in telling him just the same thing that the Parrot said." (William Temple, *Works* [London, 1720], I, 390–91.)

[46] Charles Darwin, *The Descent of Man* (London, 1871), p. 57.

[47] G. G. Leibniz, *Opera Omnia,* Tom. V (Geneva, 1768), 72.

[48] Karl Krall, *Denkende Tiere* (Leipzig, 1912), pp. 237–38.

together, as has been described by that excellent observer P. Huber, who saw ants chasing and pretending to bite each other, like so many puppies."[49]

By the way, it is rather common to experience "higher mental life," corresponding to that of man, in ants in particular. Huber, quoted above, observed an ant which by looking at the work of its fellows "came to the same conclusion" as he himself had arrived at concerning a mistake in the construction of a supporting wall in the ant-heap.[50] And the Reverend W. F. White has seen an ant, a disconsolate mourner, so affected by its sorrow that it attempted to exhume the body of a dead fellow ant which had just been buried.[51]

These examples demonstrate sufficiently clearly that it is possible to perceive a wealth of mental entities implicit in the behavior of animals and that the mental set of the observer is of the greatest importance. In this connection we may note that modern animal psychology has given up the attempt to study animal behavior in terms of this kind of psychoid entities and is instead trying to unravel the determinants of animal behavior and take its starting point from that.

There are also people who perceive psychoid entities where the mental aspect has nothing to do with anything mental in an organism. In such cases, it may then be "a former organism," as when a dead aunt communicates, for example, through the movements of a table leg, or it may be spirits, demons, and other kinds of supernatural beings, the mental life of which is implicit in the perception of a particular material sequence. Here also there are very wide limits to what it is possible to perceive.

There is in addition a more general religious attitude, which makes it possible for people to perceive the intentions of a Divine Being in different ways, implicit in the perception of things and

[49] *The Descent of Man*, p. 39.
[50] G. J. Romanes, *Animal Intelligence* (London, 1904), p. 128.
[51] *Ibid.*, p. 92.

events. Or it may be the perception of something like what H. C. Oersted called the Soul in Nature: "Innumerable as are the effects determined by natural laws in every object in nature, however insignificant it may be, so I deeply feel an infinite, unfathomable Reason within them, of which I can only comprehend by fragments an incalculably small part. In short, nature is for me the revelation of an endless, living and acting reason." [52]

In terms of the generally teleological attitude which we normally adopt with regard to biological phenomena, it is often true that, starting from this position, we perceive a variety of intentions and purposes implicit in the perception of a sequence of events. Without going too deeply into this whole question—which would remove us too far from the problems with which we are concerned—it may be reasonable to point to the role which such psychoid entities play in our perception of nature and of existence as a whole.

Finally I shall mention a special group of psychoid entities, where the psychic aspect implicit in the material aspect does not appear as having anything to do with anything really psychic. We can perceive a threatening cloud, a friendly landscape, a majestic mountain. Alfred Lehmann, in his treatise "On Moods in Nature," took a special interest in such perceptions and attempted to analyze the extent to which these moods depend on associations and previous experiences. For example, he believed it is our experience of the labor involved in climbing to the top of a mountain which makes us experience the mountain as majestic. "In other words, it only means that the feeling for the exalted in Nature, on the whole, depends on reproduced kinestetic sensations." [53] There is little doubt that prior experiences, such as those mentioned, are of importance as background for the possible perception of mood; but the actual experience of the majesty of a mountain or the friendli-

[52] H. C. Oersted, *The Soul in Nature* (London, 1852), pp. 343–44.
[53] Alfred Lehmann, "Om Stemninger i Naturen" (On Moods in Nature), *Oversigt over Det Kgl. Danske Videnskabernes Selskabs Forhandlinger* (1913), No. 5, p. 382.

ness (or unfriendliness) of a landscape does not necessarily include any memory of an earlier experience. The "soul-like" quality, which is given in such experiences, may appear completely immediate, just as directly as the friendliness of a face, for example.

Some people experience this kind of psychoid entity much more frequently than do others. Some books, such as Chesterton's, are full of them, and he often uses them with great virtuosity to create the desired atmosphere. Thus the detective, Father Brown, in the story "The Wrong Shape," speaking about an oriental knife, comments: "It's the wrong shape in the abstract. Don't you ever feel that about Eastern art? The colours are intoxicatingly lovely; but the shapes are mean and bad—deliberately mean and bad. I have seen wicked things in a Turkey carpet." [54]

Here we can also mention Ludvig Feilberg's essay "On Offensive Physiognomies in Things." [55] Feilberg appears to have perceived such offensive physiognomies everywhere, but as he clearly assumes that his readers do the same, he does not explain, in any great detail, what he means by the expression. One or two examples will show some of what he means: "Sometimes the brewery in Rahbek's Road with its sound of machines may present itself with a strong expression of personality (an offensive physiognomy)." [56] Or another example: "I am thinking of Korup's Garden in rainy weather, of the offensive physiognomy which it sometimes has when one is sploshing past. It might be as if one had left all hope behind and gasped for breath. What is the use of it all? Or the roof on Jensen's house. It may gaze at one with a pair of stereotyped eyes and a physiognomy so distasteful that one becomes quite cold around the heart. The spine collapses like a razor." [57]

We can also add that Feilberg's real interests is not to give a description of these experiences; they have a special meaning in his "philosophy of life," because the appearance of the "offensive phys-

[54] G. K. Chesterton, *The Father Brown Stories* (London, 1950), p. 92.
[55] Ludvig Feilberg, *Samlede Skrifter,* II, 3rd ed. (Copenhagen, 1949), pp. 284 ff.
[56] *Ibid.,* p. 287.   [57] *Ibid.,* p. 288.

iognomies" becomes for him the symptom of what he calls "stag-
nation in mental life."

For us this kind of perception has a special interest, because here
we have instances of psychoid entities without any perception of
the psychic aspect as having anything to do with any inner mental
life. In a friendly landscape, the friendliness is implicit in and con-
fined to the material aspect of the experience without involving any
reference to some kind of mental life "behind" it. In a friendly
face, the friendliness may also be implicit in the material aspect
without reference to anything "behind" it—and this is true in most
instances, unless we adopt a particular "set" so that we perceive it
with reference to some inner state, or unless we are forced, by
special conditions in the whole of the perceptual situation, to adopt
such a "set."

3 * On the Perception of Action Sequences

IN THE PREVIOUS CHAPTER we have surveyed a number of different psychoid entities with special reference to their importance for the perception of others and of their behavior. In the present chapter we shall discuss in detail certain problems in connection with the perception of the actions of others.

When we perceive the behavior of another person as action, a psychic aspect is implicit in the perception of the material sequence, i.e., the "intention" of the person, the "purpose" which governs the behavior, the "meaning" of the behavior pattern. In the previous chapters we have used these words rather indifferently, corresponding to the way in which they are used in daily language. In certain connections, however, it seems possible to discriminate different meanings of these words; we may, in some cases, by "intention" describe more especially the governing mental factor which we perceive in the person acting, while "purpose" is used more to indicate the aim toward which the behavior appears to be directed, the attainment of a goal. And finally, to say that behavior has a "meaning" may indicate that the behavior is directed toward a goal and is shaped in a way which may assist in achieving this goal.

However, here we shall disregard these possible differences that may occur when we perceive the actions of others, and just say that we are dealing with an action when we perceive a behavior sequence as governed by a "mental factor." We do not propose to make use of the variegated special meanings which may be found in the words "intention," "purpose" or "meaning," because it is not particularly practical to choose any one of them as the name for this governing factor. I prefer to develop a new word as the label for the psychic aspect of the perception of an action, and shall use the word *sens,* from the Latin *sensus* (the meaning of this coined word *sens* may approximate a certain meaning of the French word "sens," the English "sense," and the German "Sinn"). Therefore when we perceive human behavior as action, I shall, in the following pages, say that implicit in the perceived material sequence there is a certain *sens.* By this, I mean that we perceive the behavior as being governed by a mental factor.

When I perceive the behavior of another person, it is most frequently presented to me as an undifferentiated totality in the sense that the material sequence and the *sens* are implicit in each other. If I adopt a particular set, then I may make the material aspect stand out and may take a special interest in the question as to which movements of the body and limbs and perhaps of handled objects form a part of the perceived behavior sequence. On the other hand, I may take more of an interest in the *sens,* and then the intention, meaning, or purpose of the man may be salient in my perception of his action.

Generally, the *sens* appears in such a fashion that I perceive the intention, purpose, or meaning as being present to the acting person himself. When I see that the man wants to light his pipe, then his intention appears to me as something which is present in the individual's own perception. I see that it is part of the man's own experience. At times I may perceive him as wanting to light the pipe or to do other things without it appearing that he himself realizes his intention. Nevertheless, I perceive his intention as directed toward the same goal as in the cases where I perceive that he clearly realizes himself what he wants to do. This may happen with brief actions where we perceive that the man acts "without thinking about it," or while preoccupied with other things. But it may also happen in the case of more extensive behavior sequences when we clearly perceive the man's intentions while, at the same time, it is given for us that this intention is not present in the person's own experience. A typical case of this kind, where we perceive the purpose of a person's behavior while at the same time being certain that he does not know his own intentions, is the case of unconscious love, which, as Kaila points out, "not only is a common motive in novels or short stories, but also happens frequently in real life."[1] Here we may perceive that the person's behavior is directed at being near to the object of his love, being in her company as much as possible, and making an impression on her; and it may at the same time be quite obviously present to our perception that the individual himself does not perceive this as the purpose of his whole behavior.

This, however, is an exception. In general, we experience an intention as something present in the perception of the person acting—at least if we are at all interested in this side of things. Often the *sens* is implicit in the material sequence in such a fashion that we see the behavior as a goal-directed act without being concerned with how far this goal is present to the person's own perception while he is acting.

As we have discussed earlier on, not all behavior in others is perceived by us as "acts"; we may perceive them as expressive behavior (page 20) and then the perceived psychic aspect is not a *sens*. We do not perceive the behavior as something which the person intends to execute but as the consequence of a feeling or some other psychological state in the person; in this case the behavior is perceived not as action but as expression.

In other cases we may perceive behavior sequences as actions for which we do not perceive any *sens* as implicit in the material sequence. Such actions may appear as strange, meaningless, incomprehensible, or as governed by an intention about which we are not very clear. It may appear to us that the person has a meaning for his behavior but that we do not grasp the meaning (see page 59 about the understanding of language). In othe cases the meaninglessness may be such that we perceive the be-

[1] Eino Kaila, *Personlighedens psykologi* (*Copenhagen, 1948*), p. 298.

havior as mad. Or it may be an intermediate type of experience as when we feel that there *must* be some meaning in what appears to us as madness, so that we stand like Polonius before Hamlet with the perception: "Though this be madness, yet there is method in it."

Very often when we experience a behavior sequence as actions without a given *sens,* then the experience acquires a special character due to our lack of understanding of the other person—a character which easily shifts toward a perception that "there is something wrong with this person," at least if our own lack of background is not perceived by us as a basis for the understanding. In Chapter 4 we shall discuss how this observation is important not only in our perception of mentally ill persons but also in ordinary daily perceptions of our fellow man and his behavior.

Even if the *sens* is not immediately implicit in a perceived material behavior sequence, the behavior need not always appear meaningless. The *sens* may often be presented in a more indirect way. For example, we may see a man behave in a certain way without perceiving what the purpose is, and then ask him what he is doing; we are now told what the purpose is and therefore we know what the meaning of the behavior is—we do experience the *sens* of the behavior but it does not appear directly. Several experiences and increased knowledge with regard to the particular type of behavior will often result in the *sens* appearing immediately implicit in the material sequence. We can discover many degrees from the point where the *sens* is given directly up to situations where, from the perception of the behavior sequence itself, we are not able to experience any *sens* but may obtain knowledge of what the meaning of this behavior sequence is by other means. But let us first take a closer look at problems in those instances where we perceive the *sens* as intrinsic to the perception of the material sequence.

What is now the basis for our perception of a given action? What are the conditions for the emergence of a certain *sens,* for example the perception that the man wants to light his pipe? Why do we experience just this *sens,* and not another, for example that he wants to write a letter? The first thing we can say here is that a certain *sens* normally corresponds to a certain perceived material sequence, a sequence in which certain movements of the body and the limbs together with the handling of certain objects may form a part. The *sens* "he wants to light his pipe" corresponds normally to a material sequence which comprises certain definite movements of the arm, hand, and fingers together with the handling of certain objects—pipe and matches or lighter. The *sens* "he wishes to write a letter" corresponds to a material sequence which includes other movements and the handling of other objects.

1. On Processing Stimuli

In the case of the perception of the actions of another person, we may concentrate on different aspects of the total situation. Certain changes take place in the physical world around us; these physical processes influence our sense organs; a number of processes are initiated and result in our perceiving certain changes in our experience of the world around us. These changes appear as what I have called here an "experienced material behavior-sequence"; intrinsic in this sequence, we perceive the *sens*—the sequence appears as an action and we see what it is the person is doing.

Which actions we are going to perceive in a given stimulus-situation is not determined unambiguously by the physical stimuli alone. For instance, I have shown a film lasting two or three minutes to a number of subjects, where there appears a person carrying out a number of simple little actions, and we find that in many cases different subjects perceive different actions even if they have all been presented with the same sequence of physical stimuli. The same stimuli do not appear always to result in the same processes, so that the result becomes the same experience.

This is not only true of perceived actions. It holds for many cases of perception that the same physical stimulus-situation may result in different experiences for different persons, or perhaps for the same person at different times.

How physical stimuli will be processed depends upon a number of different factors. An important aspect of the whole process is determined by the structure of the human organism and the way the nervous system and the sense organs function; in addition, there are several other factors which may have some influence on the process and thereby on the experience. A person's earlier experience in various fields will often determine how he processes a certain set of stimuli. For example, a written statement looks different to the person who has learned to read than to the illiterate. A person's wishes, feelings, and needs may influence the processing of stimuli. From among the many investigations that American psychologists have conducted, let me just mention Bruner and Goodman's interesting, if disputed, demonstration that ten-year-old children overestimate the size of coins; the overestimation increases with the value of the coin; and the children of poor parents overestimate much more than the children of wealthy parents.[2]

In an actual situation of perception processing may be open to influences from something which we may for the time being, and somewhat loosely, call a "set"; if my set is changed, then a certain group of stimuli may be processed in such a way that I perceive something differently from what I perceived before I changed my set.

A couple of examples may make the meaning clear. If I look at a map, or even better at Rubin's vase figure, then, by a certain special set, I can change figure and ground so that the field, which before I perceived as ground, is now perceived as figure and vice

[2] Jerome S. Bruner and Cecile C. Goodman, "Value and Needs as Organizing Factors in Perception," *J. Abn. and Soc. Psychol.*, 42 (1947), 33-34.

versa. The stimulus situation is the same, but I have changed my set.

If I sit before Wundt's complication clock [3] and see the pointer travel across the divisions of the clockface and perceive the sound signal every time the pointer passes, say, division 25, then by adopting an appropriate set I can perceive the sound as being coincident with the passage of the pointer over, for example, division 18. With a different set I can shift the perceived coincidence in the opposite direction, so that I perceive the sound when I perceive the pointer as passing, say, division 32. Objectively speaking, the bell sounds every time the pointer passes, perhaps, division 27 but, dependent on my set, I may perceive the sound as being contemporary with a different passage of the pointer, lying either before or after the objectively given position.

A beautiful example of how such a set may influence the processing of the stimuli, and thereby the experience, is to be found in Rubin's experiment on the "shifting of sound." Among other things Rubin exposed his subjects to a sound stimulus which consisted of two different sounds, a dull sound like the stroke of a hammer on wood, and a more tonal sound, as from a muffled bell. When these two sounds were given in rapid sequence, separated by less than 0.1 of a second, subjects were often able to change the perceived order by adopting a special set. Using a "natural set" the stimulus hammer—bell was experienced in the order hammer—bell, but a special set to hear bell—hammer usually resulted in the subject hearing that order—while the opposite was true with the opposite order of stimuli. As a subject, Rubin himself says:

"When I say that I hear bell—hammer, then it means that first I experience the sounding of the bell, and then the sounding of the hammer. And this obtains quite irrespective of whether the objective order is

---

[3] The complication clock is made in such a way that a rotating pointer passes across the divisions (e.g., 60 divisions) on a kind of clockface; when the pointer or hand passes a certain division mark, not known to the subject, a bell sound is heard and the subject must then indicate where the pointer stood when the bell sounded. This point may be varied from experiment to experiment.

bell—hammer or hammer—bell. . . . (During the experiments I have proceeded as follows:) First I have made clear to myself the order in which I heard the sounds when using a "natural" set, and then I changed my set to hear the opposite order. Usually this was not possible during the first few trials, but demanded several repetitions. I did not give up before I had heard the order for which I was "set" definitely and with absolute certainty. Then I tried to adopt the opposite set, and in this way I changed backwards and forwards several times." [4]

The examples clearly demonstrate that a set may result in a change in perception even if the stimulus remains the same; we think that this happens because a particular set influences the way in which we process stimuli. In what follows we shall return to certain problems in connection with sets, but now let us first have a look at the process itself.

The processing of stimuli has several aspects and here we shall take a special interest in two of them. The first I call sensory processing,[5] and if we are dealing with visual objects, then it concerns among other things such conditions as the size, form, color, and structure of the perceived object; the higher the degree of processing, the clearer these variables appear in perception. A visually perceived *figure* has undergone a higher degree of processing than the background; objects seen peripherally have normally undergone a lower degree of processing than those that we fixate. Within visual perception we find many degrees of sensory processing, from the extremely low degree that corresponds to a stimulation of the blind spot to the perception of a complex pattern, for example, which is seen clearly and in great detail. Similar conditions obtain in the other sensory modalities.

[4] Edgar Rubin, "Geräuschvershiebungsversuche," *Acta Psychologica,* 4 (1938), p. 218 and *Experimenta Psychologica* (Copenhagen, 1949), pp. 324–25.

[5] In the essay "Drøm og neurose" (2nd ed., pp. 10 ff.) I have used the expression "perceptual processing"; but as most authors use the word "perception" in such a way that it must include what I call "conceptualization," I prefer in the present context to give up the use of the word "perceptual," in order to avoid misunderstandings.

The other aspect of processing with which we now shall concern ourselves, I shall call *conceptualization;* this has to do with those aspects of perception which deal with *what* it is that we are perceiving. Usually we perceive not just an indefinite "something" but what this "something" is. We see not only a particular something of a certain size, form, color, and structure, but we see what it is, e.g., a pencil. When we perceive something, it will normally be experienced as belonging to a group or a category. In the experience the object manifests itself as placed in the group to which it belongs for us in the actual situation.

Frithiof Brandt has introduced the expression *type-awareness* and differentiates between pure sensation and the perception of sensation, so that by "sensation" he means what I call sensory processing and by "perception," sensory processing together with conceptualization. "By type-awareness we then understand the awareness that the sensation is an example of a type more or less well known to the subject." [6] And this "type-awareness" is always found in perception; "to perceive a thing is to experience the thing as a type-determined thing." [7]

Jørgen Jørgensen specially emphasizes the role which the individual's set plays in the formation of concepts and thinks that it is not so much similarities between the things that determine the concept formation, but rather sets or attitudes that determine which things will be placed in the same group and thereby also determine which phenomenological similarities will become of interest in any particular context.[8]

Sensory processing and conceptualization are combined in most cases. A lower order of conceptualization often corresponds to a lower degree of processing—and by a lower order of conceptualization is meant the choice of a less specific, more general, concept. A certain degree of sensory processing is frequently the condition

[6] Frithiof Brandt, *Psykologi,* 3rd ed. (Copenhagen, 1947), II, 29.   [7] Ibid.
[8] Jørgen Jørgensen, *Psykologi paa biologisk grundlag* (Copenhagen, 1941-46), pp. 493-95.

for the possibility of conceptualization to a higher degree. We see that a person is doing something, but we have to look closer to see *what* he is doing; we hear someone say something and have to listen more closely to hear *what* it is he says.

However, it is not always sufficient to listen or to look more carefully, in order to accomplish a higher degree of conceptualization. It is perfectly possible to perceive something by employing a high degree of sensory processing and a low degree of conceptualization; this condition is particularly apparent when we are examining perception in fields where we have but limited knowledge.

Stimuli which result in A perceiving one and the same entity only may for B result in perceptual experiences that comprise very many different things, which have only a few traits in common, making it possible to place them in the same group. A city dweller may see only corn in all the cases where the farmer perceives rye, wheat, barley, and oats, all distinguished from each other by unmistakable differences; at times, children from towns may lump even more things together and call it all grass. To many people a stone is a stone and they do not experience much of a difference, whereas the geologist would find it absurd to talk about one and the same thing. And if we see a row of Chinese characters, then it is perfectly possible to experience their variations and clearly to see the shape of each character, but the differences do not mean anything to us. We can only place them in the group "Chinese characters," since the common stamp is so definitely the dominant aspect. Yet it would be rather impossible for a literate Chinese to confuse them.

To get to know a subject or a field consists to a large extent in disintegrating entities, as it were, so that what was before one and the same entity, a uniform mass, now becomes differentiated into obviously separate entities that cannot be confused. "Epistemologically, the development from child to adult," Frithiof Brandt says, "consists just in this that what is given through the senses is experienced with greater and greater specificity. And this development continues when an adult is being trained within a particular field." [9]

In many cases there is a close connection between the two aspects of processing, so that conceptualization also influences sensory processing. When new knowledge has the result that stimuli which before gave rise to a perception of a single entity now lead to the perception of two differently grouped entities, then we may perceive differences which before did not appear at all. When, for example, the city dweller learns to distinguish between the different kinds of cereals, to see wheat, rye, and barley, then the three grains will appear to have more differences than they did before. William James dealt with one side of the problem when he discussed how one learns to know the difference between entities which are very similar, as for example closely related types of wines; in this connection he says: "The names differ far more than the flavors, and help to stretch these latter farther apart." [10]

The world in which each of us lives is the result of many involved processes. We process stimuli, structure them in many different ways, arrange them in groups, and build up a world in our experience—a world which depends partly upon stimuli and partly on the way in which we process them.

We shall now return to our specific problem, the perception of the actions of other people. In our daily life it is normally quite simple to perceive the various actions, major or minor, of other people. We see the maid not as doing something indefinite but as laying the breakfast table; we see the children not as being occupied in some vague pursuit but as dressing, and similarly with the different people that we meet in the course of the day under circumstances that set us to perceive their actions. In the next chapter we shall discuss the various attitudes that we may adopt in the face of the behavior of our fellow men and the importance of these attitudes for the structure of our perception. Here we simply as-

[9] *Psykologi,* II, p. 32.
[10] William James, *Principles of Psychology* (New York, 1918), I, 511.

sume the presence of a general interest in what people are doing. Large areas of our daily life unfold themselves in a predictable manner: the situations that we experience, we have experienced before; we walk the roads that we walked both yesterday and yesteryear. In such circumstances we are in some way prepared to perceive the commonplace; we process stimuli with this attitude and we experience approximately what we usually experience in that particular situation.

But it happens that we encounter new situations, or that we observe other people acting, without being set beforehand to anticipate what they will be doing. We may then perceive a material sequence, where the *sens* inherent in the sequence is very indefinite; we perceive an action, but the perceived entity is conceptualized only to a low degree. For example, we see a man working with something, but we do not know for certain what the work is. For instance, the experimental subject LK said, after she had seen the film mentioned earlier (about the man who carries out various short action sequences): "First he sits and does something, and works on something." Another subject, KR, said about another situation in the same film: "He came in and did something or other with his coat." It is, however, rather difficult to organize experiences of this kind as the actions of others are presented to us, because the subsequent course of the action usually results in our placing the entity in a higher concept and we then see *what* the man is doing and no longer just that he is doing "something or other."

In most cases such a more precise *sens* appears quite quickly, and when it has been provided, it may influence the processing of the subsequent stimulus sequence so that, for example, certain parts of the perceived material sequence dominate, while others fade into the background. The *sens* may function in this way as an attitude or set much as in the cases described above. As long as we are dealing with a low-level conceptualization of the experienced action, there will generally be no definite structuring of the perceived material sequence; but as soon as there appears a more precise *sens,* the sequence will become structured and the *sens* functions as a set which is decisive with regard to how the processing of the subsequent sequence takes place.

That the *sens* functions as a set does not normally appear in experience; ordinarily it remains as what we call a "functional set." But in certain cases we may find something in the perception which corresponds to this set. The experimental subject, TJ, says about the man in the film: "First he placed his pipe in his mouth, then he took something out of his pocket, which I thought 'would become' matches—but it 'became' a fountain pen, which he placed on the table, and only then did he get hold of the matches." The subject perceived that the man wanted to light his pipe, and this *sens* resulted in her being prepared for him to take out the matches. As we said above, to a certain *sens* there corresponds a certain perceived material sequence: This sequence may include certain movements of the body and the limbs, and often it will comprise also the handling of certain objects. Just as the perception of the handling of certain objects may determine which will become given for us, so we find that a given *sens,* when first it appears, may influence what objects we shall experience, because it may function as a set toward processing the stimuli in such a way that these particular objects manifest themselves.

The experimental subject RV describes a part of the film sequence in this way:

At first he sat and drew—at the very beginning he sat down and took out his pipe and the matches to light the pipe. He did light it and placed the matches nicely in the ashtray. Then he took something in his hand, at first I thought it was the matchbox and thought, why does he do that? Then I suddenly thought it was a piece of eraser, because now I became certain that he was drawing, then I also thought that it looked so white. —Then the pipe went out again; then he lighted it again, and now I saw that it was a matchbox which he must have retained in his hand because he expected the pipe to go out.

The subject's perception of the object that the man in the film held in his hand is influenced by her perception of the action which the man is doing. When she perceives that the man is lighting his pipe, she perceives a matchbox. But under the influence of the subsequent sequence, where the earlier indefinite behavior becomes more firmly conceptualized step by step ("he does something, writes or draws; aha: he draws"), the previous perception of the object changes, as it becomes part of a new behavior sequence; the matchbox becomes for a time a piece of eraser, but when he again pays attention to his pipe, then the rubber in her perception becomes a matchbox again. We shall look a little closer later at the manner in which a magician systematically exploits the fact that we sometimes process stimuli in such a way that we perceive the same stimulus quite differently, depending on the behavior sequence in which the things have become parts.

The *sens* may, therefore, function as a set, which influences processing; for example, we see a man light his pipe and we process the stimuli in such a way that certain movements dominate the experience in connection with certain objects (here in particular the pipe and the matches) or we see him draw a sketch and here again there are certain movements and certain objects which are dominant in the perception, while others retire into the background.

Our sense organs are at all times exposed to a wealth of stimuli; some of these stimuli we process so that they result in experiences; and the processing may be influenced by a set, so that the set determines how the resulting experience will be structured and conceptualized. It is not a question of a single set but of a whole system of sets, which govern processing in various ways. These sets may be present in consciousness, as when Rubin consciously adopts the set to hear the sounds from the hammer and the bell in a certain order, or they may be purely functional, as when, in daily life, we process long sequences of sound stimuli into perceived Danish or English speech, but normally without being aware of the particular set that governs this process. They may be very comprehensive sets, which depend on the whole culture in which the individual has grown up, or they may be very fleeting sets that dominate in a single, brief situation and then cease.[11]

We may describe this by saying that our perceptual processes are governed continuously by such a system of sets—a system which in certain respects may remain permanently unchanged, or unchanged for shorter or longer periods, while in other respects it may be continually changing. As Postman and Bruner expressed it: "Man is perpetually prepared or *eingestellt* in one way or another and what he sees at any moment is a resultant of this preparedness and of the nature of the stimulation bombarding him." [12]

When we perceive another person executing an action, then the given *sens* may be rather indefinite to begin with, only to become more precise as we experience the rest of the sequence; and the *sens* may become the determinant of the conceptualization of what is experienced and of how further processing will take place. This processing may function selectively in such a way that certain parts are processed in a more detailed fashion and are conceptualized to a higher degree; they stand out in perception while others remain conceptualized to a low degree and do not make themselves felt in the experienced action sequence.

We have a parallel to this in the perception of language. When we hear or read a verbal utterance, the words often get their actual meaning, or as Lis Jacobsen says, their "situational meaning," [13]

---

[11] A small observation may illustrate how elusive and incidental such a set can be: Just before I alighted from the tram in front of the City Hall, I heard, without paying any great attention to it, the tones from a horn orchestra somewhere in the distance. I walked in my own thoughts along Vestergade and saw a man coming toward me carrying a horn. When I passed him, I discovered that the horn was a reading lamp and only when I began to speculate over why I first had seen a horn did I remember the orchestra. It is not unreasonable to suppose that the sound of the orchestra had created in me a sort of set with the result that I processed the stimuli from the lamp into the perceived horn.

[12] Leo Postman and Jerome Bruner, "Perception under Stress," *Psychol. Rev.* (1948), p. 314.

[13] "At any one time, in any language, it is the context that determines the meaning and only this contextually limited 'situational' meaning enters the

partly from the preceding text, which continuously creates a specific set, influencing concept formation, and partly from the immediately subsequent text, which may make it possible to translate into a concept of a higher order that which at the moment of perception was of a lower order. If I say: "In order better to illuminate . . . ," then the word "illuminate" is placed for the time being in a category of a lower order and if I continue the utterance: "In order better to illuminate the worktable," then the word "illuminate" becomes placed in a different category of higher order than if the utterance were: "in order better to illuminate the problem."

It seems that a set of the kind governing the processing of stimuli may be necessary in order that we may perceive sound stimuli as understandable verbal utterances. In his classical thesis on problems of attitude and set, J. von Kries discusses this problem in relation to the question of whether it is correct to talk about different sets when one hears (and understands) different languages. Here he says that on the basis of personal experiences it appears clear to him that one may be "prepared for" a language such as German or English, or French or Italian. "The change in the pattern of behaving is particularly clear for me when I turn my attention toward other peoples' conversation under circumstances when, initially, it can be heard but is not clearly understandable, either because of distance, or because of noise or such like. I then attempt to understand the conversation by assuming successively that they are speaking French or English, etc. The sensory apparatus is tuned to the various languages and the right setting has the effect that now a good deal can be understood while to begin with nothing was understood." This kind of change in set is made consciously, but if we stay abroad for a long time, then

---

thoughts of the person who is speaking and hearing, writing and reading (at least if he is not a linguist)—this is a rule which, if anything in the life of language can be so called, must of necessity be called a law. If this law did not obtain, all speech would be impossible, because it is not merely 5 or 10 per cent of the words of a language that are homonyms, it is, rightly considered, a very great part of the vocabulary." Lis Jacobsen, *Dansk Sprog* (Copenhagen, 1927), p. 300.

von Kries thinks that we undoubtedly acquire a permanent set in the foreign language; the set is different from our set when we are at home, but it is not constantly present in our consciousness.[14]

I myself have had the opportunity to make certain observations on sets with regard to language. The first year after I had moved to Copenhagen from my home in South Jutland, I lived in a room on the ground floor, facing the street. In the evening, just before I fell asleep, when I heard people talk while they passed on the pavement just outside, I nearly always heard them speak my home dialect, even if I did not understand what was being said. As there is no reason to think that they really spoke that dialect, the more likely explanation is that my habitual language set had taken over when I was relaxing just before falling asleep.

In several cases when I have returned home from a shorter stay in Sweden, I have observed that a newly acquired verbal set may persevere for a short time. I have, on my return home, sat in the streetcar in the evening and heard people at the other end of the carriage converse in Swedish; as soon as I listened more closely, I could hear that it was Danish that they were speaking. But on one occasion I did decide for myself after listening for a long time that they were indeed speaking in Swedish; in order to be completely sure, I went past them when I alighted from the car—and now found that they spoke quite normal Danish.

In order to investigate the problem a little further, I have made the following experiment: I played three phonograph records, each of about one minute's duration, for a number of experimental subjects. I explained that the records were made from rather indistinct radio broadcasts in Swedish, English, and Danish, and that my purpose was to investiagte how much the listeners could understand in spite of the distortions and the disturbances. The subjects were instructed to write down all that they could comprehend, even if it was just single words. Of the 31 students of psychology

---

[14] J. von Kries, Über die Natur gewisser mit den psychischen Vorgängen verknüpfter Gehirnzustände," Z. f. Psychol., 8 (1895), 6, 7–8.

who took part in the experiment, all 31 wrote down some English words (from one to 18 words), 10 wrote a more or less complete sentence each, 1 had two sentences and 1 had five; 21 persons had noted Swedish words (from 2-14 words), 5 quoted a single sentence and 1 had two sentences. Only 10 subjects wrote down Danish words (from 1-8 words), 3 reported one sentence each, and 2 had two sentences each.

All three recordings were of Danish speech, each about 175 words long (consisting of readings from Hans Christian Andersen's story "The Improvisator," read by three different persons) played backward. It would therefore seem that the experimental subjects, exposed to sound stimuli that have the character of speech, are able to process portions of the stimuli into perceived words in various languages depending on the instructions. The instruction creates an actual set toward that particular language and this set influences the processing of the stimuli.

When we perceive the behavior of other people, we may also be using more comprehensive sets which in certain respects are comparable to the sets directed toward various languages. Our set or attitude toward the actions of others may change with the social setting: We are prepared for one kind of behavior pattern in our social life, another in the office; people reveal one kind of behavior-pattern when they are at a seaside resort, another when they participate in committee meetings. In the army, in hospitals, among sailors, in school, and in many other places special forms of behavior are valid. The theater has its own special behavior, and the church has its own. In all these cases it holds that we must be set for the dominant behavior pattern, in order to perceive other people's actions clearly.

Lack of knowledge with regard to such special behavior patterns, so that we cannot adopt the right set initially, or mistakes, such that we are prepared for a different behavior pattern, both make it difficult for us to understand the behavior of others. Either we find it difficult to experience any precise *sens* at all as inherent in the experienced material sequence, or it turns out that the *sens* given is quickly contradicted by the perception of the subsequent sequence. A more comprehensive set may determine which *sens* each individual smaller action sequence may get, and if there is anything wrong with this overall set, it will often become obvious because the *sens* in each smaller act cannot be maintained but conflicts with subsequent experiences.

Altogether, the position of the *sens* during the evolving perception of an action sequence offers a number of problems of great interest, and in the following section we shall attempt to unravel these things a little further.

2. The Role of the Sens During the Perception of an Action Sequence

We shall now deal with certain aspects of the *sens,* as it appears during the development of a perceived action sequence, discussing these problems in the light of experiments, which I have conducted by showing moving pictures of small action sequences to a number of experimental subjects.

I used 8 mm film and took the films myself; the films have usually been shown to one subject at a time. I instructed the subject to look at the film and to take an interest in what the acting person does and why he does it. I added that this is not a test of memory but that one should look at the film in an ordinary way, in just about the same way as one would look at an amateur film shown by an acquaintance who had made it himself, but in such a manner that it was possible afterward to tell me, the experimenter, what the acting person did and why he did it. The films I used lasted about three minutes each.

One of the films with which I have worked a great deal showed a sequence which can be described approximately as follows: A young man sits behind a table and writes for a while; then he looks around, looking behind him over his right shoulder. He replaces the cap of his fountain pen and stands up. He bends down a little and feels with his hand into a coat which hangs on the back of the chair on which he was sitting. He straightens up again and pats the pocket in his trousers. Then he stretches out his hand and takes the pipe, which is lying in the ashtray in front of him on the table; he sits down. Now he takes the lid off the tin of tobacco which stands next to the ashtray, knocks the pipe on the ashtray and then scratches it clean. He fills the pipe, places the filled pipe on the table, stands up and puts on the coat. He puts the coat right by moving his shoulders while he takes hold of the lapels. Then he puts the pipe into his mouth and sits down.

Now he sits for a while and looks at what he has written, meanwhile hitting the table gently with his left hand. Then he reaches out and takes the matches, which are lying in front of him on the table, takes out one match which he throws aside, then another which he strikes, lights the pipe, puts out the match by waving it in the air, and places it in the ashtray. He takes the cap off his fountain pen and continues to write; then he takes the pen into his left hand and begins to draw.

He takes the pipe out of his mouth, looks at it and puts it back into his mouth, puts down the pen and takes hold of the matches. He strikes a match three times, it does not light up, he throws it away and takes another. This catches fire and he lights the pipe, places the match in the ashtray, pushes the matchbox aside, takes the pen into his left hand and draws again.

Again he sits and writes with a number of books around him; one is seen to be a book of music. He looks into the books while he is writing. He places the pen on the paper and begins to put the books together, tears a piece of paper off a pad and places it in the book on the left-hand side, closes the book and places it on top of the others. He stands up and moves toward the right-hand side of the picture, stretches into the picture, takes something on the table and puts it into the breastpocket, moves again toward the right, stretches in again and takes the pen, screws on the cap while walking completely out of the picture on the right. The chair stands empty for a moment; then he returns with a large book under the arm. He sits down and places the book on the table, opens the book, looks around in it, in a searching manner. He runs the finger down a page on one side of the page, then down the other side, holds the finger still, writes something down. He replaces the pen cap, moves first the left hand down into the coat pocket, then the right hand into the trouser pocket, then holds a packet of cigarettes in the right hand, takes out a cigarette and places it in his mouth. He moves the right hand down to the trouser pocket again, holds a matchbox in the hand, takes out a match, strikes it and lights the cigarette, shakes the match until it goes out and places it in the ashtray in front of him on the table (the ashtray is not visible), takes the book on top of the stack on the right-hand side, opens the book at the place where before he placed the piece of paper, runs the finger down the page, closes the book and moves the hand toward the point where the pen is lying.

After showing the film, I said to the subject: "Now, would you please tell me what happened in the film?" I wrote down the description, which for the most part was given spontaneously, often with one or two questions by me in the middle of the exposition. After writing down the spontaneous description, I asked possible supplementary questions and noted the answers.

The descriptions were very varied both with regard to the amount of detail in the description and with regard to the content itself. A couple of examples may give an idea of how the action sequence of the film was reproduced.

Subject EH said:

I saw a man working—isn't that all? He sat and wrote a little; he sat and did the mad things which people who study usually do. Then he needed to smoke his pipe; he stood up, found his pipe and filled it. He was a little confused and could not find the things. He put on his coat— it was not necessary, he did not have the matches in his coat pocket. Then he sat down and began to work again—and then only did he light his pipe. Then he wrote a little—then he began to draw with his left hand, why I do not know, perhaps he is left-handed. Then his pipe went out, the first match did not work, and then he got mad at it and threw it far away. The other caught fire and he placed it neatly in the ashtray. Then he got a whole lot of books to help him. But then he had to use an even larger dictionary and there was no room for it alongside all the other books. Then he puts them away and fetched the large dictionary—then he opened it and found what he needed. When he had finished with it, then he puts all the books together, stood up, took his fountain pen and left.

With these words the subject completed her spontaneous description and I asked: "When the man stood up to fetch the dictionary, did you then expect him to come back again?" The subject: "Yes, because he did not put the books away; he only made room for something else."

Another subject, JT, said:

A man sat and worked at his writing desk. He appeared very busy—that became obvious both when he lights his cigarette and his pipe, and when he fetches a dictionary. He gets up in a hurry and he strikes matches with great urgency.

First he sits and writes; when he gets up the first time, I say spontaneously to myself: 'he wants to get hold of his pipe' and it was true. (Experimenter: "How did you know that?") I don't know why, it was in the unconscious, as it were.

When he stood up and put on his coat the first impression was that he would leave. When he began to feel into the pockets I thought spontaneously about the pipe—I would do it in that way. First he took down into one pocket, then into another. Did he not take the pipe from the pocket? He did at least take something to smoke from the pocket, either one or the other.

Then he sat down to work again, wrote with the left hand. It struck me: he is drawing something or other. Later he got up again. Again I thought he would leave the room, but he comes back with the dictionary. (Experimenter: "What did you think when he came back, since you had expected he would leave?") I thought that I must have been mistaken.

He sat and followed the columns of print with his finger, until he suddenly found the answer—on the top half of the right column, at the right-hand side.

Then he feels in the pocket again; I thought about the pipe again, but he takes out some cigarettes instead. It looked as if he did not get the cigarette lighted with the first match, but he did it in the end. Then I say to myself: 'By Jove, he did do it after all.' Then I don't know— was there anything else? (Experimenter: "How did the film end?") Well, that is quite indefinite, didn't it end with the man sitting and reading in a book which he had lying before him? (Experimenter: "What was the last picture?") The man was there in it—I think. Was he?

The subject added spontaneously: "What did the man's work really consist of—I have no impression of it." And finally the subject said: "Now I remember, he took the pipe out of his coat pocket, and then he scrapes it out, fills it and puts it in the mouth and lights it." (Note that the subject earlier in his description was doubtful whether the man took the pipe from his pocket.)

The first scene in the film (where the man sits and writes) is described in a remarkably identical way by the majority of the subjects; 34 out of 44 began their reproduction of the course of the film: "He sits and writes." Of the remaining 10, one says that he draws, another that he works, while 4 begin with a sort of survey of what happened in the film, and 3 begin by talking about how the man appeared: busy, upset, nervous; a single subject began by pointing out that he had not experienced a coherent motivation for the whole story.

That the man at the beginning of the film sits and writes (or perhaps draws) is perceived by all subjects, including those who do not say so in the very first sentence. This is an action they know well and it proceeds fairly uniformly for a sufficiently long time interval, so that the *sens* can form: what is he doing?—he sits and writes.

For most of the subjects it also holds that this action may be apparent without it being absolutely necessary to perceive a specific motive in the person acting. As ER expressed it: "First the man sits and writes; the whole situation is for me a quite ordinary action, which does not need a reason, neither in his case nor in mine."

The given *sens* "the man is writing" may now function as a set, which among other things influences how stimuli will be processed. This becomes clear when the man stops the writing movements and does something else. In a number of cases it happens, therefore, that the subject goes on processing the stimuli using the set which corresponds to the original *sens* "he is writing." The material sequence changes but the subject still experiences the same *sens;* the man in the film is still seen as intending to write something, and when he gets up from the desk, it may be in order to fetch a book which he needs for his writing; some subjects thus described their experience.

A given *sens* does not change immediately when the material sequence changes. Processing continues in line with the original set, until the sequence, as it were, forces a change, because it is no longer possible to process stimuli so that the sequence can be experienced in a way corresponding to the original *sens*. Then a new *sens* will form, corresponding to the change in the material sequence, and stimuli are then processed corresponding to a new set determined by it.

The new *sens* does not always form at once. There may be a transitional period where the given *sens* is rather indefinite; the experienced action is an entity placed in a concept of a low order. We see the person doing something, but not what he is doing. And only later, as the sequence develops, will the experienced event undergo a revaluation and be placed in a higher category, so that we again see what the man is doing.

The original set results in our processing stimuli in such a way that the experienced entity acquires a definite, firm structure. In the transitional period where the action sequence present is conceptualized to a low degree only, the perception is also structured to a low degree only. The new *sens* gives an attitude, a set, which in turn leads to a firm structuralization of the experienced sequence. For example, the subject BR says: "Then he stood up to get hold of his tobacco." (Experimenter: "How did you realize that?") "I didn't see it at once. He stood up to fetch something or other, looked for the pipe, found it, looked, I think, for the matches also. Then he lighted his pipe and sat down to write again." And another subject, JS, says: "Then he stands up and looks for something or other. It looked as if he had lost something. It turned out to be his pipe."

The translation from one *sens* to another, when one observes an action sequence in another person, does not normally stand out very clearly in perception and may be difficult to comprehend. This is because the new *sens,* when it becomes available, acts backward as it were, so that what was perceived immediately previously as placed in a concept of low-rank order, now appears as placed in one of a higher rank order; the entity is given with a stamp of having been present. We experience that the action which now is evident to us was really present much earlier, but it is only now that we realize what the action was that we experienced before. As ETR says: "He wanted something, I didn't know immediately what it was; then I saw it was the pipe he was looking for—one fills in backward also." And PK describes what he experienced: "Then he takes out the pipe and now it all of a sudden appears as if he just before had searched for the pipe in his coat."

This retroactive reordering of experienced entities often results in the low-ranked part of the perceived sequence not becoming present in the experience. We really perceive that we did indeed see him all the time carrying out the action with which we are concerned. And 20 of the 42 subjects, who mentioned the episode with the pipe, describe that particular part of the action sequence such that they move directly from the writing situation to the pipe situation, without an intermediate stage in which they do not know what the man is doing. In their reproduction of the experience the one *sens* takes the place of the other immediately without any part of the sequence being described in terms of a low-ranked concept. Even if there had been a time where they only saw that the man did something vaguely (but did not know what it was), this perceptual condition is no longer available to them, now that the higher ranking has taken place. JT, whose description of the film we quoted above, gives a very clear example of this condition when he says that when the man in the film stands up, he spontaneously said to himself: "He wants to get hold of his pipe." He experienced clearly enough that he has seen immediately what the man's intention was. And when the experimenter asks how he could know that it was the pipe the man wanted, the question does not undermine his perception that he knew all the time the man's intentions —and that in spite of his inability to explain how he could know beforehand. He can only say: "I do not know why, it was the unconscious, as it were."

Such retroactive rankings take place all the time when we experience a behavior sequence. They may, as we have shown, happen because of what we see the person doing during the subsequent sequence, but also other factors in the whole of the experienced situation may be of importance. If it concerns an action sequence in which there are several persons, then the way in which we experience the behavior of each of them may be influenced by what we see the other persons as doing. This condition is also important with regard to the problem of retroactive ranking. Let me illustrate this with an example: In one of my films a lady appears standing at an easel and painting a picture. Another lady goes over to a low table at the side, on which some painting gear has been placed. She takes a brush and cleanses it in a bottle with turpentine standing on the table, and then she leaves. A little later the painter goes over and takes some paint from a tube in her box on the table. It now appears that most of the experimental subjects have a rather uncertain perception of what the lady was doing when she cleansed the brush. "She did something or other, I cannot see what it is," LH says. "She mixes up the painting things—

cannot see what she is doing," AMG says: "Then she walks over
and pushes some colors or brushes about, I cannot see what it is,"
ETR says; and others express themselves in a similar fashion.

But for some of the subjects it happens that this behavior, which
in the experience of most of the subjects appears as low-ranked,
becomes very highly ranked because of what they perceive the
painter as doing a little later in the sequence, when she fetches some
paint.

We find AL describing that particular part of the film in the
following way: "The other woman goes over to the chair where
the paintbox with the tubes is standing—takes out a new tube, unscrews the top and makes the tube ready. The painter leaves the
easel, goes over to the chair, takes the newly opened tube, squeezes
out some color onto the palette and walks over to the easel again."

It is reasonable to think that, like other subjects, AL has perceived that the lady did something or other with the painting
things when she rinsed the brush. At the moment the subject sees
the painter taking the paint from a tube, this "something or other"
becomes retroactively ranked, so that the subject now perceives
the action of the lady as consisting in putting out the tube, ready
for use.

When we perceive the behavior of others as action sequences,
there is a tendency to process stimuli in such a way that the experienced situation becomes a coherent whole; if several persons
appear, then the perception of the behavior of one may determine
how we shall perceive that of another. The final perception is
determined by the whole of the structure of the given situation
and most frequently in such a way that it does not appear to us
afterward that retroactive rankings have taken place.

It is generally true that if we have arrived at an understanding
of what another person is doing, then we frequently perceive that
we have seen him doing it all the time. When an entity appears
as highly ranked, it may be difficult to remember that just previously it was already present but ranked very low. But also in

cases where it is evident to us that the action at first was ranked lower, and then during the later sequence became more highly ranked, we may still perceive that we have been dealing with the same entity all the time: we saw somebody else do something and now we know what this something was.

This obtains not only with regard to the perception of actions but also with regard to all perceived entities. If an entity is present, at first ranked in a lower category and then in a higher, then, at the transition from the lower to the higher ranking, we perceive that we now realize what the more indefinite entity was which was present initially. If I see a small animal running across the field, without immediately seeing what kind of animal it was, and I then hear the animal mew—well, then the small animal I saw was a cat. We may here refer to what Tranekjær Rasmussen says about what he describes as "complete-able" entities: If an entity appear to us as "complete-able," and if step by step it does become complete before us, then we are dealing with the same entity at all stages of the process. If we are concerned with an entity which after the process may appear in our experience as immediately given, then this identity (this being the same) may be immediately given.[15] We can also here mention Metzger's observations in connection with his investigations of shadows cast by rotating rods.[16] Under certain circumstances, when the shadows of two circling rods are moving across a screen, a two-dimensional movement is seen: the two shadows move toward each other, coincide, and move away from each other again. This experience then changes in such a way that one sees a circling movement in space of two rods, at a fixed distance from each other. When this change takes place, one may experience that what one originally saw "really was" the circling movement, which is now seen. The shad-

[15] E. Tranekjær Rasmussen, "Besvarelse af den bundne skriftlige seks Ugers Opgave i Konkurrencen om Professoratet i Filosofi ved Aarhus Universitet" (manuscript, 1938), kap. 4.
[16] Wolfgang Metzger, "Tiefenerscheinungen in optischen Bewegungsfeldern," *Psychologische Forschung,* 20 (1935), 209.

ow picture makes possible both experiences, and when the observer has perceived the circling movement, then he also perceives
that this is really the one which had taken place all the time.

If we now consider how subsequent events in the film appeared
to the experimental subjects, we find that the new action, "the
man is lighting his pipe," is perceived as very simply motivated by
most people. He wants to smoke, and then he lights the pipe; there
isn't really any need for any further rationale in the perception of
this action. However, when he later begins to write again, with
the consequence that the original *sens,* "he is writing something,"
reappears, then we find in many subjects a tendency to rank the
lighting of the pipe as a part action of a more comprehensive action
situation, so that the smaller sequence does not break up the larger
sequence but becomes a part of it. The smoking of the pipe may
under these circumstances be perceived as motivated in such a way
that it somehow seems to belong to the work of writing, which the
man is doing. The movement which the man makes may still have
the *sens* "he wants to light his pipe"; but this action may be experienced as forming a part of a wider context so that the *sens* is
no longer simply that he wants to light his pipe in order to smoke,
but that he wants to smoke for a definite reason—for example, in
order to write better. It is therefore no longer a matter of a single,
independent action but of a part included in the whole sequence.

Tendencies to incorporate the smoking of the pipe in this manner, as a part of the whole situation, appear in a number of experimental subjects. A typical example is given by AB: "First he
had to write a letter, but it really looked as if he couldn't find the
inspiration. Then he thought: Perhaps a smoke would help?
Apparently it worked because he then began to write again." Another, JK, places the smoking in the total context so that he experiences: "He apparently works best with tobacco." In other subjects the connection between the smaller action situation and the
more comprehensive one may be somewhat looser, and they may
perceive, for example, that he stops because he has finished a

paragraph or section of his work and now needs a short pause, which he then fills by smoking.

When we perceive the actions of others, there appears in many instances to be a tendency to preserve a given *sens* for as long as possible. When we perceive a certain intention in the acting person, it does not seem obvious that we will perceive a new intention as soon as a change has taken place in the material sequence. And where the unfolding of the sequence makes it possible, it may also happen that a smaller action sequence may be placed in a more comprehensive sequence, so that the *sens* is expanded, as it were, but not changed into a new *sens*.

Until now we have considered cases where the *sens,* when it is present in perception, has turned out to be congruent with the development experienced subsequently. The subjects first perceived that the man sat and wrote, then that he wanted to light his pipe, and the material sequence corresponded to this; i.e., the stimuli could be processed in such a way that no conflict arose, and so that no mistake was experienced, of the kind: "I thought he would do one thing, but it turned out that he did something else." There were, however, some indications of such a sense of mistake, i.e., in the cases where the subjects first perceived that the man wanted to fetch a book or something else needed for his work and realized thereafter that it was the pipe he wanted to get.

There is, however, in the film, a situation that gives a possibility for more detailed investigation of what takes place when the further observation makes it difficult to maintain the given *sens.* That is the part of the film where the man stands up, puts on his coat and then sits down again. This sequence, that the man stands up and puts on the coat, is such a change in the material sequence that for many, but far from all, it has the result that the preliminary *sens* is insufficient and a new *sens* arises. There are, however, a number of subjects who maintain the *sens* "he wants to light his pipe," and they process the experienced sequence on the basis of the corresponding set, so that they succeed in perceiving the actions of the man in putting on the coat as a part of the action of lighting the pipe. This is done by perceiving that the man puts on the coat because he has the tobacco, pipe, or matches in the coat pocket and thinks it easier to search the pockets when he wears the coat.

In a few cases experimental subjects process the stimuli on the basis of this set, so that they see the man take the matches or the pipe from the pocket after he has put on the coat. (In the film the pipe, the matches, and the tobacco are on the table in front of the actor.) But most frequently the perception is formed in a different way. The subjects do not see the man take something from the pocket but, on the contrary, they perceive that the man thought he had the matches, or something else, in the coat pocket and that it was for that reason he put on the coat. In this way the subjects avoid a conflict that might arise between the given *sens* and the subsequent events.

Let us now look a little at such a situation: I see a man put on his coat because he wants to get his matches from the pocket; the subsequent sequence has the result that I see him take the matches lying on the table in front of him. I have therefore made a mistake: the intention of the man in putting on the coat was not to get easier access to the matches. Far from it—not I, but the man himself made a mistake. His intention was exactly the one which I experienced and when the movements he made did not have the intended result, then it was because he made a mistake. I experience his behavior as directed toward the aim of getting hold of the matches, and when the action does not have this result, then I experience that the person is wrongly orientated with regard to the position of the matches; he is acting from wrong premises, so that he does not reach his aim—but I myself have made no mistake.

In such cases it is as if we defend ourselves against an experience of having made a mistake. We maintain the currently available psychoid entity, the action of the other person as it manifests itself to us. As long as the perception remains immediately given and we simply see what the other person is doing, without it occurring to us to speculate about whether we have seen correctly or not, the responsibility for what we perceive as mistakes and stupidities during such an action sequence is attributed to the acting person; in most such cases it is quite evident immediately that the other person is acting in a not too useful fashion. For example, EH says: "He put on his coat, it was not necessary, he did not have the matches in the coat-pocket." And JS says: "For a moment I had the fleeting thought that it was stupid to put on the coat in order to get hold of the matches."

In some cases the perception of the actions of the other person is accompanied by a certain reflection, but as long as it is only a consideration of *what* the man is doing and *why* he is doing it, and not a concern with whether one is right in one's perception of what he is doing, then the result will mostly be that one perceives the other person as behaving in an unreasonable way. "I wondered why he put on his coat, as the sun was shining in the room," ET said. "But I suppose there was a tobacco pouch in the pocket—but he did not need to put it on for that reason." And BG says: "Perhaps it was only in order to search for the matches—did he think it easier if he had the coat on?"

A particularly clear example of the tendency to place the mistake on the person acting, and thereby to preserve the given *sens* and to avoid the experience of having made a mistake oneself, is given by AJ. She perceives that the man puts on the coat because he wants to take the matches from the pocket; the experimenter asks where the matches were, and she thinks he had them in his trouser pocket. The experimenter then asks further, if she perceived that she had made a mistake with regard to the reason that he put on the coat, and she answers: "No, he puts on the coat because he thought the matches were in that pocket—he shook his head in an irritated manner, as if he discovered that they were not in the coat and was annoyed about it." Because of this perception, stimuli were processed on the basis of the operating *sens* so that the mistake was made by the person acting and the *sens* was preserved.

It may also happen that the subject, after he had begun to process stimuli on the basis of an attitude corresponding to the *sens* "he wants to get hold of the matches," then gives up this *sens* instead of perceiving that the man made a mistake. For example, IJ says: "I thought it was because he wanted the matches that he got hold of the coat, but instead he puts it on." And as mentioned above, it is only a minority of subjects (7 out of 44) that perceive the sequence in such a way that the behavior of the man when he puts on the coat is a part of the action of lighting the pipe. That a few of the subjects do perceive that the man puts on the coat as a part action of the lighting of the pipe may perhaps be due to the action earlier on in the film when the man was looking for the pipe and did feel into his pocket while the coat was hanging on the back of the chair. The *sens* "he wants to take something from the pocket" may have been prepared by the behavior experienced earlier. Often, when we perceive others, we have a set that the person will repeat what he has done before; and we also find, as we shall discuss in detail below, that a *sens* which at one time has been present in perception may raise its head again and make itself felt again.

For a greater number of experimental subjects (18 out of 44) the experience of the material sequence, of the man standing up and putting on the coat, resulted in a new *sens* arising, i.e., that the man is about to leave. They perceive that he has finished his work and now leaves the room. It may happen that the *sens* for a moment may act retroactively and include the pipe situation, so that this is perceived as belonging to the departure action; he has finished writing and lights his pipe while he is leaving. As SS expressed it: "Now he lights his pipe and puts on his coat in order to leave." The placing of the perceived entities in the appropriate concepts seems always to tend toward creating as firm and clear a connection as possible in the perceived action sequence.

The film itself, however, shows that the man, after he had put on the coat, sits down on the chair again. It is therefore difficult to avoid that the *sens* "he wants to leave" comes into conflict with the further perceived sequence. Two subjects have, however, avoided the conflict by processing stimuli in such a way that they really perceive the man as leaving. In the reproduction of what they have seen the man do, they "move" the action of putting on the coat to the end of the film and then perceive that the film ends by the man leaving. Subject IC finished his description by saying: "And then he put on his coat and left."

Traces of such a tendency to "regroup" the experienced sequences under the influence of a given *sens* is also found in subject CB, who saw the film twice. During the second showing he exclaims spontaneously when he sees the man put on his coat: "Really, is it already now, I did not know that, I thought it was at the end." When CB saw the film for the first time, he perceived that the man put on his coat to leave; he did not know for certain what the ending of the film was, but thought that the man probably stood up and went out at the end.

In subjects who perceive that the man puts on his coat to leave, we find attempts to preserve the *sens,* similar to those that we found when the coat situation was placed in the pipe-lighting action sequence. Also in this case there are subjects who "make" the actor make a mistake, instead of perceiving that they themselves have committed an error. They perceive, for example, that the man wants to leave, but then he discovers that he has still a little time left or that he has forgotten something. Later in the film when he gets up and walks out of the picture and returns immediately with a large book, many subjects experience it in the same way. They saw him walk out to leave the room; a single subject processes the stimuli in such a way that he perceives that he disappears, and that it is another person who comes in, when he returns. But apart from this, it is also common for subjects to perceive that he really does want to leave, but then has forgotten something, or there was something he had to look for at the last moment, and so on. In all these cases the *sens* is maintained; the subject does not experience that he has made a mistake; no conflict arises between the *sens* and the sequence experienced later.

In certain cases the conflict between the given *sens* and the later sequence may lead us to give up attempting to find a meaning in the behavior of the person acting. ER said about the situation when the man has fetched the large book: "What took place was clearly that now he had to leave, he also had to remember his fountain pen. Then it occurred to him that there was something he had to look up at the last moment; but then it all turned meaningless when he sat down and wrote on." The subject has perceived that the man wanted to leave and when he then did not do so after all, no new *sens* arises; hence the man's behavior appears meaningless. Such an experience of lack of meaning may result in the subject suddenly realizing that "it is only a film." In a couple of cases the subjects remark that it is of course not a real situation, not even a "real film," but only an experiment; in other words there is no need to see any meaning in the behavior of the person, as perhaps there *is* no meaning. ER says when he perceives the behavior as meaningless: "It has probably been of importance that I knew that it was a contrived situation; had it been a real situation I would probably have looked for another set."

It also happens that subjects just simply forget the coat incident. For example, CN says: "I had forgotten that he puts on the coat." (Experimenter: "What did you perceive when he put it on?") "Then I thought that he would leave, but that he didn't do." In these cases, if there has been a *sens* producing a perception that the man wanted to leave when he puts on the coat, then it has probably been placed in a concept of a low-rank order so that the giving up of the *sens* does not result in the subject perceiving that he has been mistaken. It is possible that in everyday life, when we experience the behavior of others without having a special set to experience why they do what they are doing, we then often forget a *sens* which becomes refuted by the subsequent sequence before it becomes placed in a concept of a higher order.

But for many subjects the observation of the subsequent sequence, when the man sits down again after having put on the coat, results in it now appearing that they have made a mistake. This produces something very specific with regard to the way in which the psychoid entity, the action of the other person, manifests itself in experience. The entity ceases to be an undifferentiated whole; the material sequence and the *sens* are no longer intrinsic to each other. The *sens* does not appear immediately; it is formulated as a kind of hypothesis, which is then rejected. HT says about this: "When he puts on the coat, then I see that he wants to leave; when he then sits down, I become very surprised and realize my mistake, and then I conclude more consciously that it was because he was cold." And TS similarly says: "First I expected that he would leave, when he puts on the coat, and only when he sat down and went on working did I make up the explanation that it was because he felt cold. The first explanation, that he wanted to leave, is an immediate expression; that he felt cold, I should call a construction." Others express themselves in a similar way.

Such a perceived mistake may therefore have as a result that what was at first experienced as a psychoid entity, where *sens* and the material sequence were inherent in each other, now more or less becomes dissolved; one realizes that the *sens,* which seemed to be present as something that one saw, was really something that one only thought. It is not that subjects always say that they first perceived that the man wanted to leave as given and then realized that it was only something which they inferred; very often their description takes the form: "First I thought he would leave but then he sat down." As AC says: "Then he puts on his coat; I thought it was because he had to leave, but then he sat down again, so it must have been because he felt cold, this I thought afterwards." Here, where the perceived action "now he is about to leave" has been present as a highly ranked concept, there is no retroactive ranking taking place, no re-ranking, as we have seen above when the previous sequence has been placed in a low-ranking concept.

When one perceives that the person stands up to do something undefined, and when one then a little later sees him take the pipe, one rearranges the concepts retroactively and perceives that it was the pipe he wanted to get hold of all the time. But when one perceives that he puts on the coat in order to leave and afterward figures out that it must have been because he felt cold (as 13 of the 18 subjects did who thought that he wanted to leave), then nothing happens to support the perception that one saw, it was really all the time because he was cold. The ranking of the perceived entity cannot be changed in this way; the experience must first be canceled, as it were, by the psychoid entity being dissolved in a material sequence and in a *sens* which appears as a mistake, while at the same time being isolated from the material aspect of the experience. Then a new *sens* is created which normally does not appear as something immediately given, but more frequently seems to be the result of an act of deliberation, even if in many cases probably a quite fleeting one.

In the subjects who at first did not experience that the man was about to leave, or where this *sens* at least did not stand out clearly in the experience, the *sens* "he puts on the coat because he is cold" appears quite immediately. And we see how this *sens* also in such a case may function as a set which influences the processing of stimuli. For example, KBD says: "He was shivering a little, he felt cold, apparently." And ER: "When he puts on his coat, I thought it fitted into the later sequence; he shivered a little as if he felt cold." A good example of how this *sens* may influence the processing of the stimuli is given by SF, by the way in which she experienced a small blemish in the film (consisting of a small wavy shadow at the very edge of the film). She says: "It looked as if there was an enormous draught through the window (so that the curtain was billowing in the wind). It was only when he had put on the coat that I experienced it as draught through the window, at first it appeared to be a blemish in the film." It is also the case that the coat situation with this *sens* appears as an action which is completed at once and does not affect the subsequent sequence. He puts on the coat in order not to feel cold any longer and this is the end of this action. The subsequent sequence does not need to proceed in any particular manner for the *sens* to be preserved, as would be the case when one perceives that he puts on the coat in order to leave. Unless he directly does the opposite and immediately takes the coat off again, there is no great risk of this *sens* coming into conflict with the subsequent sequence.

When the *sens* "he puts on the coat because he feels cold" is not immediate but is the result of deliberation, then no such set is created to determine the processing of the stimuli. HT says as follows: "It was like this, he did not enjoy to put the coat on, as one does when one feels cold. That he felt cold was a construct, it really was—I was all set to find motives because of the instruction."

When as the result of the perception of an action sequence a *sens* must be given up because further events have refuted it, it may nevertheless not cease to function. It is as if it is kept ready and begins to function again as soon as events give it an opportunity to do so. Subject JS gives an example of how the *sens* "he wants to light his pipe" is given up for the moment when the man gets up, only in order to make its influence felt again when stimuli are processed in such a way that the *sens* does not come into conflict with the subsequent sequence of events. JS says: "Then he found the tobacco, filled the pipe and I expected that he would light it at once. I thought for a moment that he would stop working and leave, when he put on the coat. But then I thought that the window was open, because the light was so strong and that he felt cold. Then he found that he had the matches in the pocket of the coat." And even in the instances where a refuted *sens* does not make itself felt again immediately, as in this case, it may still exercise some influence on how the subsequent sequence is experienced. When the man put on his coat, the subject ME perceived: "Well, now he is leaving; but as he sat down again, then I thought at first that it was because it was cold in the room and that he felt cold; but a little later I rather got the impression that he had to hurry out." To the question by the experimenter, why he did get this impression, ME replies that it was because of the man's hurried way of working. Later in the description ME said: "It rather looks as if he is preparing a lecture which he is about to deliver and he is in a hurry to finish." We see here how the perceived action becomes the form under which a more comprehensive sequence manifests itself; this can also be found in other experimental subjects. For example, JK said: "Perhaps he had to go and read a paper about his investigations."

In many cases it looks as if the perception of how the film ended has been influenced by the *sens* "he wants to leave," which may have arisen and been denied again during the subsequent sequence, both when the man stood up and put on his coat and later when he stood up and walked out of the picture, only to return at once with the dictionary. Many subjects, among them EH, whose description we have reproduced above, say that the film ended by the man standing up from the table and leaving. In the film the man is still sitting at the desk and working in the last picture, and the film ends abruptly without any kind of final action. When we experience the behavior of another person as an action sequence, there takes place a process of retroactive ranking of the experienced psychoid entities; as we have shown above, that which a moment ago was ranked in a lower order, now becomes more highly ranked, and we then see what it is the other person is doing. When the film finished suddenly in the middle of an action sequence, then the last part of the perceived sequence may be present in the experience, but placed in a low-rank order, so that the subject does not quite know what it really was that the man was doing at the end. As one subject expressed it: "The last actions were spoiled, as it were, by the interruption of the film."

We now postulate that the *sens* "he wants to leave" still exercises an influence in a number of the experimental subjects, and at the moment when the film is interrupted it exercises an influence on the processing of the end of the sequence, so that the subject perceives that the man at the end walks out. In order to investigate this problem a little further, I took an interest in how the subjects perceived the ending of the film. I asked 44 subjects altogether with special reference to this question; in the cases where the subjects did not spontaneously express themselves about the film ending I asked: "And how did the film end?" The subjects' answers are divided as follows:

"He leaves"	15, about 34%
"I think he is leaving"	6, about 14%
"He stands up, puts the books together, replaces the dictionary"	11, 25%
"He remains sitting"	11, 25%
"Don't remember"	1, about 2%

A third of the subjects, therefore, experience that the man finally leaves at the end; and if we include those who thought that he leaves but are not absolutely certain, then we include about half of the subjects.

Now we cannot just assume that the subjects perceive that the man leaves at the end because earlier on in the film they have perceived "Now he wants to leave." An attempt to estimate from descriptions whether such an experience has been present produces only rather ambiguous results; and to ask directly would be to run too great a risk because of the suggestion involved. By itself it is quite possible that the subjects have a general need to experience a sort of "reasonable ending," an action which indicates that the film is now over. At the showing of another edition of the film which ends in the same way, one of the subjects, EL, answers the question on how the film ended: "He was still sitting there; he just disappeared in the middle of all his papers and things. He could just as well have stood up and indicated in some way or other that he had finished; but perhaps there should be no ending."

I undertook a special series of studies in order to investigate a little more closely whether it was an earlier perception of the man as about to leave that made subjects perceive that he did leave at the end. I excised the first few scenes of the film, so that the new version begins with the man standing up and putting on his coat, and I also removed the scene where he stands up and fetches a book. The result was a film where he sits down the whole time. This edition of the film should not result in the subjects getting the experience that the man wants to leave. And if the hypothesis is correct that it is such a *sens* which causes the experience that he does leave at the end, then the subjects seeing this version of the film should not experience that the film ends by his leaving the room.

I have shown this new film to 28 experimental subjects and focused upon their perception of the end. In this case the answers are divided as follows:

"He leaves"	0, 0%
"I think he stood up"	1, about 4%
"He closed the books"	3, about 11%
"He continued to sit and work"	20, about 71%
"I don't remember"	4, about 14%

Here we do not find that subjects perceive that the man leaves at the end, and 20 of the 28 say directly that he remains sitting at his work. The result strengthens the assumption that in the first version of the film it is a *sens* originating from an earlier part of the experienced sequence which influences the processing of the ending and results in the perception that the man leaves the room.

When we perceive the actions of other people, we process stimuli on the basis of a set corresponding to the given *sens*. And it seems that it is not only the current *sens* which may influence the set but also a prior *sens* which even may have been refuted because it came into conflict with the sequence as perceived later. If once we have perceived that a man is doing something, then it is not enough that he stops doing it and does something else—at a moment where circumstances make it possible for us, we shall still be inclined to perceive that he is executing an action which we saw earlier on that he intended to carry out. This may perhaps happen as soon as the sequence reaches a point where the present *sens* becomes rather imprecise and the perceived action therefore is reduced to a low-ranking concept so that we do see the man as doing something, but don't quite know what he is doing. The earlier *sens* may then generate in a set through which the action will be ranked in such a way that we now see him doing what we experienced him as wanting to do before.

Under certain conditions this sort of thing may play an important role in our perception of the behavior of others. It may have special importance for the psychology of eyewitnesses. If one has to decide upon the reliability of a description by an eyewitness, there could be good reasons for taking an interest in whether the event which took place and is now being recapitulated by the witness may have given rise to a *sens* of the kind discussed above. Even if it has been refuted by the subsequent sequence, such a *sens* could have influenced the final processing and therefore have influenced what the witness has perceived. For example, if a man has acted in a threatening manner against another man in such a way that other people have had the perception "Now he is going to attack him," then the chances are greater that these people will experience his later behavior as an attack than had his earlier behavior not given rise to such perception.

When we are dealing with experiments on the viewing of films made of short "nondramatic" action sequences, such as the ones described earlier, it will mostly be the actual sequence itself which determines the *sens,* the intentions and purposes which we experience in the acting person intrinsic to the material sequence. In our daily dealings with other people it will often be somewhat different. There it often appears to us that we know a person's intention beforehand, so that we really know what he will do even before we have seen him doing it. And if the actual material sequence perceived does not agree with the *sens* given before the event, we may still perceive that this is really what he wants to do. The acting person may then appear to us to be sly or something like that. In other cases, as in the film, we may perceive him as really executing the action which seemed to us to be what he intended to do, as soon as the sequence gives us the opportunity to process the stimuli in that way.

As long as the stimulus sequence arising in our experience of the behavior of another person is of such a kind that a given *sens* is immediately determined by the perceived material sequence, and as long as the subsequent events give rise to no conflicts, then there will be no real possibility for a *sens* springing from an earlier part of the behavior sequence to influence the processing of the stimuli. Only when the stimuli weaken, or become less dominating in some other way (with the result that the actions of the persons manifest themselves as but low ranked), would such a *sens* be able to make itself felt and gain some influence on the manner in which conceptualization will take place and on what we shall experience the other person as doing.

This condition, which we have discerned as operating in the perception of the actions of other people, appears similar in certain respects to what Gestalt psychologists demonstrated in a number of investigations of the perception of visual figures. In his exposition of the problem, Koffka differentiated between external and internal organizing forces which play a role in processing stimuli when we experience a visual figure. Internal forces tend toward a mode of processing that results in the experience of the simplest and most regular figure, while external forces counteract this pressure toward regularity and tend toward a mode of processing that results in a perception more dependent on the stimulus pattern. When external forces weaken, for example, by stimulation being very brief or of very low intensity, then internal forces dominate in the processes and we see simple, regular figures even if irregular figures are exposed. If we experiment with afterimages, where the stimulus is removed following an exposure and we are dealing therefore with an aftereffect only, the result is even more obvious: When the stimulus does not exercise a direct influence, the inner forces in processing gain more influence and the result is that we experience a regular afterimage even if the original stimulus was an irregular figure. When external forces, which are dependent on stimuli, are weak, then the processing is determined to a large extent by inner forces that are inherent in the processes —at least according to the way Gestalt psychologists formulate the matter.[17]

The situation wherein stimuli are weakened and an earlier *sens* has a tendency to gain influence over the processing of stimuli and hence co-determine how we perceive the action of another person is in many ways similar to the phenomena discussed immediately above. But there is, however, a difference that should be stressed: The inner forces with which we are dealing in our case definitely seem to be determined by the earlier experiences of the individual— at times by the immediately prior experiences, in contradistinction to the inner forces at work during the perception of figures, which are assumed to be determined by the structure and function of the nervous system.

When we observe the actions of other people, it is therefore the given *sens* which to a large extent determines how we process stimuli—and therefore what appears in perception. As we have seen, the actual *sens* may be determined not only by the immediate stimuli but also by earlier experiences; this may result in discrepancies between what we experience and what "actually" takes place (as determined by appropriate methods). Such a disparity between a "real" event and the perceived action is produced systematically by the magician. He plans his behavior in such a way that he determines how the audience will process the stimuli and he does

[17] K. Koffka, *Principles of Gestalt Psychology* (London, 1936), pp. 138 ff.

it so that we, as far as certain parts of the behavior sequence are concerned, "see" him do something different from what he "really" does.

For example, he makes certain that the *sens* in a particular, short action sequence appears clear and definite by demonstrating the specific action sequence several times in succession: he throws an orange up in the air four times, with the result that we experience clearly what he is doing when he makes the movements belonging to the throw. We become completely "tuned" to the processing which corresponds to this *sens* and when he throws the fifth time we also see the orange fly into the air—even if he holds it hidden in the other hand. Three times in succession he drops a florin into the hand of a member of the audience and asks the man to close his fist as fast as he possibly can; each time he maintains that the man is not fast enough so that it must be repeated; the fourth time he drops a penny into the man's hand. This time he is satisfied with the speed and asks the man to raise his closed fist so that all the people present can see it. When he then touches the raised hand with the magic wand and asks the man to open the fist, the florin has mysteriously changed into a penny.[18] The magic wand creates an effect whereby the audience perceives the change of coins as taking place at the moment when the wand is brought into action, instead of perceiving that they made a mistake when they saw that the man had the florin in his hand because the coins had, in fact, been exchanged earlier on. The expert magician uses his wand all the time in such a way that he controls the *sens* which the audience must experience as part and parcel of his behavior. He puts down the wand and takes it up again every time he needs to let go or to get hold of the things which the audience should not see him handling. On the whole he uses the wand to determine the *sens* in so many ways that the wand must be regarded as the most important of all the magician's tools.[19]

[18] Hoffmann, *Modern Magic* (London, 1894), pp. 161–62.
[19] Ottokar Fischer, *Das Wunderbuch der Zauberkunst* (Stuttgart, 1929), p. 33.

The magician's main problem is to create by his behavior a *sens* in the persons forming the audience such that, at the critical moment, they perceive something quite different from what is "really" going on. This he succeeds in doing by dividing his behavior into two, as it were. When we are observing the behavior of another person under normal conditions, we perceive the whole person as forming a part of the action; his speech, his looks, his movements, all are part of the action. The magician utilizes this fact and practices a division of his behavior so that his speech and eye-movements become the form under which the actions that he wishes us to perceive manifest themselves, while his hands simultaneously work independently;[20] hence, this part of the stimulus sequence is not processed so as to become part of our experience of his action. Such a division of behavior, which results in only a part of the stimulus sequence being processed to experience, is more easily accomplished if the magician himself experiences the *sens* which he wants to manifest itself to the audience. In this way he supports the specific set that has to govern the processes of the spectators, by forming the behavior sequence himself from the same point of view. He must in one sense experience himself as possessing the power to make the coin disappear from the one hand, only to let it appear in the other—and to disregard, as it were, that the removal happened in an ordinary way some little time before. And this is true not only of individual tricks but of the magician's whole appearance. As long as the magician is on stage, he must himself believe in his mystical powers; he must force himself not to think of the plain and ordinary means he must use to obtain his results and he must believe himself that the effect is due to magical forces, at least so the English magician Hoffmann maintained.[21]

What we experience is to such a large extent co-determined by the sets that govern the processing of stimuli that the magician may indeed be able to make the spectators see "anything" happening before their eyes, if he really is able, in some way, to make his

[20] Hoffmann, *Modern Magic*, p. 4.   [21] *Ibid.*, pp. 502–3.

public believe that he is a wizard possessing mystical powers. The Austrian expert in the field, Ottokar Fischer, maintained that it is this ability to create a comprehensive set that "everything is possible" that is the "real secret" of well-known great magicians.[22]

The magician is not the only one who utilizes the principle that behavior may be controlled in such a way that a *sens* arises in the audience that results in stimuli being processed so that we experience something quite different from what actually takes place. The actor does it in his own way. He too must produce a behavior which creates a definite *sens* in the public so that we see him execute actions which he does not really carry out.

Actors cannot really love, kill, deceive, save each other, in the way that they must seem to be doing. Their problem is to plan their behavior in such a way that the desired *sens* arises in the audience and so that spectators process stimuli in such a way that the love, murder, deceit, or salvation dominates our perceptions of the sequence of events—all within the limitation that is created by the general set that this is play-acting and not reality, a set which itself may be more or less clearly apparent as a part of the experience.

The actor may also use the special set recommended by the magicians, of believing himself in his artifices. By persuading himself that he loves the girl and murders the rival, it will become possible for him to control his behavior so that the spectators also experience the passion and the murder. This specific manner of acting has been treated in detail by the great Russian instructor Konstantin Stanislavskij, who strongly stressed this method at the expense of all other methods, and indeed regards it as the only possible method.

With the help of what Stanislavskij calls "the magical if," the actor must enter into his role and "live in" it; he must act as he would do if he really loved, murdered, etc. All the time he must experience the *sens* of his behavior. "Everything you do must have a very definite reason and a very definite intention and lead to the

[22] Fischer, *Das Wunderbuch der Zauberkunst*, p. 43.

next step," Stanislavskij's spokesman in the book says to his students.[23] The actor needs to experience the situation in such a way that both the reason why he does it and the intention of his behavior is clear to him while he is acting. It is undoubtedly a very important problem for the theater that behavior always takes place in such a way that the *sens* is given immediately and clearly in the perception of the spectators. If the behavior sequence is of such a type that no *sens* arises in the spectators, i.e., that they experience the behavior as meaningless, then this will not usually result in their perceiving that there is something wrong with the person acting—as it does in everyday life. In the theater it will produce an effect such that the "illusion dissolves" and the audience suddenly have perceived that, of course, it is not real but only play-acting—just as some of my experimental subjects reacted when they perceived that the man in the films behaved meaninglessly. (See page 102 above.) As long as the onlooker understands and sees immediately what people are doing and why they are doing it, then the general set that this is theater may fade into the background in his experience. But if his perception is that the actor's behavior is meaningless and that he does not understand at all what they are doing, then there will often be a resulting perception: "I cannot see what it is they are doing, but of course it isn't real, just play-acting." There are very good reasons therefore for stressing, as Stanislavskij did, that every action must be done to some purpose,[24] and we can add: in such a way that this purpose manifests itself in the experience of the spectator.

There are some actors who are able to act in such a way that even very small details in their behavior pattern become the form under which much more comprehensive acts manifest themselves, acts which do not "really" take place. We see, all the time and quite immediately, what he has done just before—for example, that

---

[23] K. Stanislavskij, *An Actor's Work with Himself,* Danish translation (Copenhagen, 1940), p. 59.
[24] *Ibid.,* p. 54.

the actor just came in through a particular door—and what he will do just after the present scene—for example, sit down and read; and it is not even necessary for these actions to take place on the stage or in the film. Whether this effect is more easily or better produced by Stanislavskij's method or by a more conscious technique akin to that of the magician is another question.

But it is of course not only a question of small details of this kind within the sequence; the actions of the actors must always be perceived as being parts of the greater entity that is formed by the story of the play, the whole action sequence that the author wishes us to experience. This Stanislavskij wanted to attain by instructing the actor to use his imagination, to absorb into his own life what has gone before and what is going to follow after, and all the time to maintain this unbroken line while he is acting.[25] In this way, by maintaining a very comprehensive *sens,* the actor can make certain that the audience experiences his behavior on the basis of the same overall *sens,* so that each single, small action at all times becomes a form under which the more comprehensive action sequence manifests itself.

There is little doubt that Stanislavskij's ideas in many ways have been beneficial to the theater; it is quite a different question as to whether he was right when he thought that there was only one correct method for creating a certain *sens* in the spectators, which is for the actor himself to experience this *sens* and to let his behavior be determined as far as possible by the *sens* as it appears to the actor himself. But what does it really mean to say that the actor must act as if he really had lost some valuable object and now is looking intensely for it? It means that he must act as he would normally act in a similar situation in everyday life. And Stanislavskij maintained that the spectator, who sits and observes what the artist is doing on the stage, quite automatically must get the feeling that the connection and the sequence of his actions take place just as mechanically as we unconsciously execute them in everyday

[25] *Ibid.,* pp. 395 ff.

life. Otherwise the spectator will not believe what takes place on the stage.[26]

It looks as if Stanislavskij wanted to create a genuine theater by making the norms of everyday behavior the accepted norms for play-acting, and in many cases this may undoubtedly be very useful. The actor is able to act his role if he completely absorbs the situation: the norms for play-acting are thus available from everyday life. And the spectator can follow the play which unfolds according to norms that he knows well from his own daily experience.

But Stanislavskij was to some extent inclined to mistake behavioral norms of everyday life as he knew them for laws of human nature. He said that he wanted to teach his pupils to behave on the stage as human beings—nonartificial, natural, purposeful, free, and unfettered, as demanded not by the conventions of the theater but by the natural laws of living human beings.[27] As we shall see later in another connection, it is not at all uncommon to mistake accepted behavior norms as laws of human nature; for Stanislavskij the mistake had the result that he did not realize that what he wished to put in place of the "theater-manner" was also a kind of "manner," i.e., a mode of acting that belongs to daily life—which probably would be much better in many cases. But it was probably not justified to demand that his mode of acting must be the only one to be used. If we regard the main purpose of the theater (but this is debatable) to give the spectators the richest possible experience, then any kind of acting would be valuable which expands, deepens, and enriches the *sens* given for us while we see the play unfold before us. And thus the behavior pattern of everyday life is not the only one that can be used; it is possible for the theater to use with advantage methods that are reminiscent of the methods of the opera and the ballet with their very stylized forms of behavior, each following their own quite definite rules. There is little doubt that certain actors at times use a technique

[26] *Ibid.*, p. 236.   [27] *Ibid.*, p. 80.

whereby they consciously shape their behavior relative to the *sens* that should arise in the public in such a way that they succeed in giving the audience a richer and fuller experience of the story and the actions than would be possible by a "natural, living, human, everyday behavior."

The theater, then, does not speak the language of everyday life, but its own language, and in fortunate moments this may result in the theater giving us a wealth of experience that everyday life but rarely offers.

4 * On the Way in Which Other Persons Appear in Our Experience

1. On the Importance of Our Attitude to Other People

IN OUR EVERYDAY dealings with our fellow men the extent to which their mental life is inherent in our experience of them varies considerably. A number of factors are important in this connection. There are great differences in how "expressive" people are: in some it is one kind of behavior, in others another kind, which reveals their personality to us most clearly. And the whole context of which the behavior forms a part may be decisive: if we see a man open a door, we probably perceive little of his mental life implicit in this material sequence; but if we see him assist his ladylove into his new car, it is possible that much of his inner life will appear clearly in our experience of him.

There is still another factor that is decisive: our attitude when we experience other people. The attitude that we adopt toward the people around us may be of great importance with regard to how their mental life will appear to us. We may act in many different ways when we experience the behavior of other people, and, depending on our attitude, the mental life of other people may be given in a more or less detailed manner, more or less "in focus." There are many attitudes that can scarcely be distinguished from each other, but at the one extreme we find a rather "defensive" attitude to the mental life of others, so that we defend ourselves, as it were, against being aware of their mental life and attempt to avoid experiencing what people are doing, what they think and feel, what they want and wish to do. It seems that certain kinds of anxiety may lead to such an attitude, whereby one processes one's experience as lowly as possible in various ways in order to avoid mental conflicts.[1]

Here we might also mention that in American psychology, in connection with the study of the relationship between needs and perception, there have been investigations that have touched on these special problems. C. W. Eriksen has conducted a number of experiments, the results of which indicate that needs that are not accepted by the individual may function in the direction of the creation of perceptual defense against stimuli that are related to these needs (need-related stimuli) according to the investigation. He showed pictures of simple social scenes to his experimental subjects, who were all mental patients, and he found tendencies in the direction of a higher perceptual recognition threshold—or other perceptual disturbances—when he showed scenes of people in the process of expressing or satisfying a need which appeared unacceptable to the experimental subject himself. Such needs he attempted to determine by association-tests. For example, subjects with an unacceptable need for aggression found it difficult to perceive what takes place in a picture of two men attacking each other with knives in their hands, or the subjects saw something other than what the picture really presented.[2] It is possible that different kinds of "perceptual defense" may be exercising an influence when we do not clearly experience the actions, expressions, and "stamp" of other people, or when we experience something different from what is "actually" present.

At the other extreme, with regard to attitudes toward the experience of the mental life of others, we find a set to experience everything others do as the form under which something psycho-

[1] Franz From, *Drøm og neurose,* 2nd ed. (Copenhagen, 1951), p. 44.
[2] C. W. Eriksen, "Perceptual Defense as a Function of Unacceptable Needs," *J. Abn. and Soc. Psychol.,* 46 (1951), 557–64.

logical about the other person is manifesting itself. This is particularly common in situations where we are strongly interested
in what the other person is doing because it is of importance to us
ourselves. The greater the importance of the decision made by
someone else for us, the more we incline to perceive his ideas,
feelings, and intentions as being implicit in every detail of his
behavior, details which under other circumstances would be regarded as accidental and unimportant. The lover who is not certain
that his emotions are reciprocated may perceive every facial expression, every movement of the hand on the part of the beloved, as
the manifestation of a positive or negative attitude, of acceptance
or rejection. In like manner one whose future is in the hands of
another may experience the feelings, emotions, and thoughts of
the other person as apparent in the smallest details in that other
person's behavior, for example when one is applying for a job, or
sits for an examnation, or stands in the court before the judge.

In the paranoic person we may find this attitude carried to the
extreme. Such patients may, as Freud observes,[3] invest the smallest
details in the behavior of others with the greatest importance; they
interpret them and make them form the basis for far-reaching conclusions. Freud mentions as an example a paranoiac who concluded
that everybody in his surroundings acted in accordance with a
conspiracy because the people in the railway station at the time of
his departure had made certain movements with one hand.

Between these two extremes we find a number of attitudes that
range from a general lack of interest in the people about us to
the greater or smaller interest in the mental life of others which
normally dominates us when we ourselves share in the action situation in which others take part.

There is nothing against our also experiencing the behavior of
other people as actions in cases where we take very little real interest
in them. This we do, for example, in traffic situations in the street,
and in trams, shops, and offices. In this way we may observe the

[3] Sigmund Freud, *Gesammelte Werke,* Bd. 4 (London, 1941), p. 284.

behavior of those people that concern us only insofar as we find ourselves close to them, pass them by, and so on. The behavior of such persons may appear to us as actions, but as long as we remain disinterested, the experience would usually be ranked very low, and we do not perceive very clearly what they are really doing.

But it does of course often happen that we do take a modicum of interest in the behavior of others in cases where we do not have to adapt ourselves to their behavior. We observe them with what I shall call "play-acting interest"; we perceive them almost as actors, and their behavior may be processed as highly ranked actions, where the *sens* is provided precisely by the perceived material sequence. Such an attitude may be "impartial" in that we experience the action sequence without an evaluating attitude, without taking sides between the acting parties; or the attitude may be "partial" when we approve or disapprove of the actor's actions, expressions, stamp. The transition from such an attitude to one which we adopt as "co-actors" may be very flexible and need not always influence the way in which we experience the mental life of others.

It does not seem of decisive importance whether we participate in the action situation or not, but rather whether we participate in such a manner that our personal status is affected—whether what takes place is of importance to our self-esteem, whether we perceive the action of the other person as positive or negative toward ourselves in such a manner that we can speak of what Sherif called "ego involvement."[4] Such an involvement of our ego and its status will usually mean (much more than the purely external participation in the action situation) that we perceive the mental life of the other person in a special way which is different from the way in which it appears to us when we take the role of the spectator and experience the actions from the point of view of interest in such "play-acting."

These changing attitudes to our fellow man play an important

[4] Muzafer Sherif, *The Psychology of Social Norms* (New York, 1936), pp. 176 ff.

role in the way in which we perceive the mental life of others as exhibited through their behavior. This is also apparent in my experiments with cinefilm, even though, in the order of things, the variations in the attitudes of the experimental subjects cannot be as rich as those we find in daily life situations. If we limit ourselves to the experiments with single subjects that I have described in the previous chapter (where the subject after having seen a short behavior sequence in a film tells the experimenter what happened in the film), then we find that this method results in virtually all the subjects taking an interest in the doings of the actors in the film; what I would call "play-acting interest." But I have also carried out some group experiments where a film was shown to a group of persons who then were instructed to write down a description of what happened in the film, what the actors did and why they did it. Here we find that the subjects' attitude to the sequence of events in the film has varied greatly. I quote first a description where the film has been experienced from the point of view of a general neutral, descriptive attitude. The subject JW writes:

We see the tower of the Church of Our Lady, the time is five to three in the afternoon. On a roof nearby a girl stands painting at an easel, she is painting a picture of the tower. Another girl stands nearby leaning against a chimney and looking at her; she walks out of the picture and the first girl remains for a long time, engrossed in her painting. The other girl comes into the picture again and walks over to a small table where there are placed some colors and takes up a bottle, removes the lid, screws it on again and shakes the bottle and replaces it in the paint-box. I did not understand the deeper meaning of this. She leaves, and the first girl stands alone again and paints a little, then she walks over to the table, takes a tube from the box, squeezes a little color onto the palette. Walks back to the easel. She gets her hand full of paint from the palette. A third girl comes and looks at the painting, they greet each other and talk a little about the painting; the second girl comes and they all three stand and discuss the picture. No. 2 girl gives a rag to no. 1 girl, so that she can wipe her hand and when that has been done she says good-day to no. 3 girl by shaking her hand. Then they all laugh about it. No. 2 girl has gone out again. No. 1 girl leaves and no. 3 girl looks at the picture alone. No. 1 girl returns and shows a few other pictures to no. 3 girl; she gives one to no. 3 girl, who puts it in her bag, but then regrets she has accepted it and hands it back again.

Descriptions of a kind similar to that of JW are common, but there are descriptions which deviate strongly from this type. The shortest is given by AH, who writes: "In the film a female painter was seen and some spectators. One bought a picture, the others did some other apparently unimportant things."

A similar description, equally aloof, but with a little more detail, is given by GH:

The film begins with a picture of the tower of the Church of Our Lady. Then the camera turns to the roof of a house which lies a short distance away from the church. The roof is flat and one sees some young ladies—apparently from an art-academy—moving around up there. One of the ladies is painting a picture of the church tower. She is interrupted a couple of times by some of the other ladies, who come and say good-bye. From the roof one can see quite a few roofs, covered with tiles. The film finishes with a picture of the church tower. The film was rather worn. And the cutting from the tower to the rooftop had been rather clumsily done.

A number of subjects experience the film in another way so that the "inner life" of the actresses is evident to them from their behavior. For example, AL writes:

Two women stand on a rooftop in front of the Church of Our Lady. One of them stands at an easel carrying a canvas on which she is painting. To begin with the other woman stands idle and looks on—it rather looks as if she is giving advice. The picture shows the church tower, the time is just about 3 o'clock. For a while I noticed the artist's activities only, then the other woman all of a sudden walks over to a chair, where the paintbox with the tubes of paint is lying, takes out a new tube, unscrews the top and puts out the tube ready for use. The artist leaves the easel, walks over to the chair, takes the newly opened tube, squeezes the paint out on the palette and walks back to the easel. After a couple of brush strokes she uses the finger. The painter is blond, perhaps brunette, rather stout. The other woman is slimmer, and I do not notice her character. Suddenly a third, dark-haired, woman enters into the picture. She has a bag in her hand and is very hearty. She wants to shake hands with the two previous ladies, first with the passive spectator—but obviously on the orders of the painter this one gets busy, fetching a clean rag so that the artist can remove the paint from her fingers before she shakes hands with the new lady. The artist now shows the new lady the picture on the easel, then some canvasses with or without a frame which stood on the chair (one of them shows a female portrait). The new woman looks very enthusiastic about all the pictures, but selects one which she quickly takes and puts into her bag. But now the artist comes with a frame and apparently wants to take back the selected picture in order to frame it—and she gets it—and the two women seem to agree on the time when the picture will be ready and can be collected.

In one series of experiments I gave a specific instruction that in their description the subjects should attempt to provide an assessment of the characteristics of the three women. This resulted in a special attitude with regard to the perception of the action sequence of the film; some definitely avoided the problem and informed us that it is nearly insoluble; but others adopted a specific set to perceive the actions of the three ladies as the data through which the character traits of the three women manifested themselves. A rather typical example can be found in SSN's description. He writes:

I perceived the first of the three women as an artist who had chosen a beautiful subject from the roof of a building here in the neighborhood (the experiment took place on the roof of the laboratory): The tower of the Church of Our Lady. The other lady I perceived as her assistant, but was rather uncertain with regard to what she really had to do and what her job was. The third lady came and visited the artist during her work and I perceived her as a lady with some understanding of the visual arts. She looked critically at what no. 1 had painted, and when the artist left the easel—out to the right, very convenient—I regarded no. 3's

action of putting one of the pictures into a bag as an expression of klep-
tomania. However, no. 1 comes back and when no. 3 realizes that she
has been seen taking the picture, she tries to save the situation by pulling
the picture out of the bag quite openly and discussing with the artist
whether she may have the picture. (Now when I sit and write this, I
become uncertain whether this is correct—was it not rather that she
took out the picture so as to be able to remark: "I can take this picture,
can't I?") As an expression of general permissiveness towards no. 3,
no. 1 lets her have the picture following some hearty exchanges (it
rather had the character of a common type of 5 o'clock "hentea titter").
By the way, there was a strange intermezzo when no. 2 could not shake
hands with the newly arrived "art critic" but first had to dry her hand on
a rag. Doesn't no. 2 like no. 3? Did she deliberately intend to cut her but
was prevented from doing so by the artist? This one appeared to me to be
more immediately sympathetic. My impression of no. 1 was the most
indistinct of the impressions which the three ladies and their behavior
made on me. I interpreted no. 3 as a lady who wanted to make herself
more important and more refined than her character allows her to. This
was how I perceived the situation—but I must confess that the outlines
in it were so indistinct that there was room for wide divergencies in
each of the judgments. (Was that intentional? Was that the idea?)

We see that SSN in his description takes a particular interest in
the actors' mental life, their motives, feelings, and psychic traits;
these things dominate the description of the film to such an extent
that we do not get any real recall of the sequence of events which
is assumed to be known, as it were.

AG gave an interesting example of how strongly a subject in
such an experiment may be engrossed in the "inner life" of the
"actors" appearing in the film; this subject had participated in a
series of experiments with the general instruction to take an interest in what the persons did and why they did it, but without
the specific instructions to discern character traits of the ladies.
She handed in an ordinary neutral description of the same type
as that of JW, but two days later she came on her own initiative
and gave me the following description of the ladies appearing in

the film, saying that she had become so interested in the persons in the film that she wanted to write something more about how she perceived them and she thought that it could perhaps be of interest to me to see how her experience had taken form.

The three ladies I shall call the artist, the friend and the guest. To begin with the artist made a rather bad impression on me. She appeared to me a little too forced; but before long she had my sympathy because I now saw her to be keen on her work and in high spirits, and her interest in the picture she was painting "rubbed off on me," as it were; very likely she would be the dominating, active and probably slightly protecting partner in her relationship with her friend who walked around doing things. She is the one who talks while the woman friend listens, she is the one who acts while the friend is allowed to fill in the smaller details.

The friend appears immediately sympathetic, quiet, subdued, a naturally flattering background for a more vital and merry nature. Perhaps she has been without great understanding of the other person's work to which she did not pay any particular attention, but I assume that nevertheless she would have been full of enthusiasm for her friend's products, just because she likes her and wishes her all possible success from the depths of her heart. That the two were very close friends I deduced from the intimate atmosphere on the sunny roof. They were there together without speaking apparently without noticing each other, as only very close acquaintances or good friends can be (or complete strangers perhaps also, but what would two ladies who were complete strangers to each other do on the same roof? The artist's presence could possibly be explained but the friend could not possibly be a person appearing accidentally but had to belong in some way).

Then the third lady, the guest, comes on a visit. The friend meets the guest halfway in a friendly manner and puts out her hand, but the guest ignores it, aims directly at the painter at the tripod and demonstrates her overpowering interest. Her behavior offended me and I did not like her. I thought it was a pity for the friend who had been overlooked. The friend took it nicely. She seemed accustomed to this kind of treatment.

The guest was very "gushing" and discussed the picture with the artist, who happily took out some pictures and I suppose the guest has overpraised and flattered her and demonstrated her own—probably—none-too-well-founded knowledge of the arts! Happy because of the interest and the favorable criticism, the artist then wanted to give one of her pictures to the guest and the guest also accepted it. Nevertheless she refused rather forcefully, and I suspected that she really did not like the picture. However she had now got stuck on her own praise and this she attempted to avoid. In the end, however, she did put the picture into her bag under pressure from the artist, who presumably experienced the refusal as modesty on the part of the guest. Much to my disgust I see a little later the guest pull the picture out of the bag again and hand it over, this time without much ado. She really would not like to have it and finally this seems to have dawned on the artist.

Even if the picture had been a dreadful mess, one cannot behave like that, and in particular not when one just before has been running over with praise. But of course this was what one could expect from a person like the guest. Nor was her entrance in agreement with ordinary accepted behavior.

I was very angry with the dark lady after a while and I get angry again when I think of her and her behavior.

She is of the kind who rubs shoulders with those who know a little beyond the ordinary, she throws flattery around. She is totally inconsiderate of those from whom she can gain nothing by being friendly to them. And how little her flattery and pseudo-interest does mean is easily seen from the way in which she refuses a well-intentioned gift.

Most likely the artist has not seen through her and praise is always nice to hear.

The friend appeared to have accepted her.

When a short behavior sequence such as the one shown in the film can result in a perception of the acting persons and their mental life such as the one given by AG, it is because the personality structure of the subjects themselves is of the greatest importance in determining how the perception will develop. In many cases our own mental set plays an essential role in how we shall experience others. In this way a person's own mental qualities may exert a great influence over the processing of stimuli when he perceives the behavior of others as the expression of traits in their personality. And when the stimulus sequence is of the kind shown in the film, sufficiently vague to permit several interpretations, then, to use Koffka's expression from the perception of figures, it becomes possible for "the inner organizing forces" to exercise a dominating influence on the experience of the acting persons, their actions, expressions, and stamp.

However, in this essay I intend to limit myself to more general variables in our perception of other people, and we shall not therefore discuss the huge and interesting field of problems concerned with the way in which the individual's particular personality traits, both normal and pathological, influence the perception of other people and their behavior.

Perhaps we should just mention that in more recent studies of personality an interest has been taken in the hypothesis that our perception of social situations can under certain circumstances be determined to a large extent by mental factors in ourselves. But the point of view of these studies is different from the one which we have adopted, because attempts were made to draw conclusions with regard to certain traits in the subject's personality on the basis of the perception of such social situations.

Among the various attempts that have been made to use such techniques both in research and in the clinic, Murray's Thematic Apperception Test is of the greatest interest. Experimental subjects are here presented with a series of pictures showing one or more persons and are instructed to tell a story about each picture. On the basis of what the subjects say about the pictures, one then tries to find hidden factors in the personality. The test is based, Murray says, upon the well-recognized fact that when a person interprets an ambiguous social situation he is apt to expose his own personality as much as the phenomenon to which he is attending.[5]

---

[5] Henry A. Murray, *Explorations in Personality* (New York, 1938), p. 531.

2. On the Way in Which the Mental Aspect Manifests Itself

As I have said, we shall here limit ourselves to the more general problems that we meet when we study the conditions surrounding the perception of the behavior of other people. And we shall now look a little more closely at the way in which a person appears to us in the perceived situation of which he is a part.

When we perceive the action of another person, we are dealing with a psychoid entity, a certain perceived material sequence, and inherent in the sequence a given *sens*—the intention, meaning, purpose of the behavior; the entity has a material and a psychological aspect. Now there are great individual differences in the ways in which the psychological aspect makes itself felt when the entity manifests itself for us in its undifferentiated totality. As we have discussed above, our own attitude plays an important role in this connection. If we are not specially interested in the mental life of the other person when we observe his actions, then the *sens* will often be given as something which determines the situation of which we perceive the acting person as being a part, and only if we adopt a more specific attitude will we experience the *sens* of the action as a form under which the man's intention, will, wishes, and so on manifest themselves. It is true of many of the people with whom we come into only fleeting contact that we perceive their actions as determined by the situation—as is also often true of the actions carried out by persons with whom we have more intimate relations. Commonly the action appears determined by the situation in such a way that the "independent" intention of the acting person is given, at best, in a very vague fashion.

Under these circumstances we perceive behavior as determined by the structure of the situation in which the person is acting; we judge that he acts as "one" always does in that particular situation.

For example, we see a man walk along the pavement: he gives way to people he meets, walks around those who walk more slowly than he does; he reaches a pedestrian crossing, waits for the green light, walks across the street, reaches a bus stop, stands and waits. When the bus arrives, he enters, finds an empty seat, looks out of the window. In our perception of this sequence the *sens* may have been given clearly enough. First: he is walking somewhere; then: he is walking along to get the bus, perhaps with a retroactive ranking so that we perceive all the time that he has been on the way to take the bus. But the *sens* manifests itself as determined by the situation, by how "one" acts when one takes a bus, rather than by a perception of the acting person's "independent" wish or intentions.

Let us now look at another example: I see a farmer pull a cart out of the barn; he closes the doors and leaves the cart in the farmyard, then walks to the stable and fetches the horse, places the harness on the horse, leads it out in the yard and puts the horse to the cart, climbs up into the cart, places himself in the seat, takes hold of the reins, gets the horse going and drives out of the farmyard. The whole of this rather complicated action sequence with all its many details can appear for me as determined by the situation, provided I am acquainted with it; this is the way "one" behaves when one harnesses and drives a horse. The man's mental life as a determinant of the behavior is present in my perception of the behavior sequence only to a vague degree.

When we perceive other people in situations like this, their inner life may then manifest itself to us to a very limited degree only. Edgar Rubin stressed this condition particularly when he considered what is evident for him of the mental life of his fellow-passengers in a bus: In general they sit there and, so far as we are concerned, they are beings without content. What passes through their heads, their concerns, their feelings, and the moods dominating them, of all this we know nothing. Yes, not only this—we do not even reflect upon the fact that something is taking place in their mental life.[6] Now it is of course obvious that Rubin's example is an extreme one, because the behavior sequence *to sit in a bus* is normally unlikely to be perceived as an action, unless one adopts a specific set to perceive it as such. All things being equal, it also seems that in the case of patterns of behavior that unfold in a monotonous way (without any variations) the mental aspect appears less often than it does in cases where the behavior sequence may change.

As I said above, the difference in the way in which the psychological aspect of a perceived action will appear, depending on the development of the behavior, becomes obvious only if we do not adopt a specific set to perceive the mental life of the other person; if we do adopt such a set, the psychic aspect of the experienced psychoid entity will in most cases manifest itself very clearly. How great a role this plays in this connection can be seen from the instances mentioned earlier (see page 62) of the extent to which some people have been able to perceive mental life in animals, when they were set to do so.

But if we do not adopt this set and if we know the situation well of which we perceive somebody to be a part, then we may perceive his actions in such a way that his mental life appears very vaguely; his action is given for us as being determined by the whole situation in which we see him. It is here of the greatest consequence how broad a situation is given for us. When a situation is experienced as not being a very comprehensive one, behavior which does not manifest itself as determined by the situation may very well be perceived as determined by a situation perceived as apparently more comprehensive, i.e., when we perceive the momentary situations as forming a part of a more comprehensive action sequence.

In our first example, of the man who took a bus, it would follow

[6] Edgar Rubin, "Bemerkungen über unser Wissen von anderen Menschen," *Experimenta Psychologica* (Copenhagen, 1949), p. 29.

that if we only perceive him as a man who is about to walk somewhere, then we could not incorporate into this sequence the fact
that he also stands and waits; but if the situation is broader so
that we perceive him as on the way to the bus, then his whole
behavior can be understood by us in terms of this more comprehensive situation. Similarly in the example of the farmer who
harnesses the horse: if only a limited specific situation presents
itself, then the variations in his behavior do not follow from the
situation; but if we perceive the whole situation comprehensively,
then the man's total behavior manifests itself as actions determined
by the total situation.

It is probably the fact that we may perceive the actions of other
people as determined by action situations, so that the psychic
aspect of the psychoid entity manifests itself very vaguely implicit
in the experienced material sequence, that has served as the starting point for behaviorists when they attempted to describe human
behavior without reference to anything mental and to create a
psychology which does not concern itself with mental phenomena.

There can be little doubt that under certain circumstances this
method for describing the behavior of others as determined by the
external situation in which we perceive them can be the clearest
and most suitable one because a large part of our experience of the
behavior of others is just "behavioristic" in this sense, and corresponding to this, it can be reasonable to accept what Wolfgang
Köhler calls "agreement with what is sound and justified in
behaviorism." [7]

But in order to be in a position to experience and describe the
behavior of another person as being completely determined by the
situation within which the action takes place, we must know
what situation is psychologically present; and not only the narrow
"stimulus" situation but the total situation to the extent to which it
can be hypothesized to influence the development of behavior. And
it is necessary to know as far as possible what the situation is for

[7] Wolfgang Köhler, *Gestalt Psychology* (New York, 1929), p. 260.

the behaving person himself, if we hope to understand his behavior as completely determined by the situation. In practice this
is not normally very difficult as long as we are dealing with "stan-
dard situations," like the ones mentioned in our examples, but if
we concern ourselves with more complicated or more special conditions it may quickly become impossible to determine what the
situation is to the acting person himself. And if we maintain as
the starting point for our understanding of the behavior of another
person the situation which is available to us, without considering
that quite a different situation may be available to the acting person himself, then such type of behaviorism may not bring any
clarification but rather confusion with regard to understanding of
the behavior of others. This does not prevent such a method from
being the ideal one for psychology to aim at—but if it is to be
carried through at some time in the future, then psychology at that
time must be almost all-knowing with regard to all the factors
which may influence the behavior of man.

But if we now limit ourselves here to how we actually *perceive*
the behavior of other people, then it is of course true that we often
do not interpret it in this "behavioristic" manner. And it is not
merely when we adopt a specific set that the mental aspect of an
act manifests itself clearly to our perception. It is often the case that
we see people do something or other which does not appear to us
to be determined by the situation in which we observe them. If
we see a man who is crossing the street suddenly turn about and
walk back the way he came, then we do not normally perceive
this action as determined by the stimulus situation; he is doing
something which for us does not follow from the situation in
which we observed him.

In many instances when a sudden change of this kind in the
material sequence takes place, we perceive the person in such a way
that the psychological aspect of the action as a psychoid entity
manifests itself in a special way. We perceived that he was walking
across the street, and when he then turns around, we do not feel

that we have made a mistake. We perceive a new *sens* that the man changed his intention; and this new intention, which is not simply perceived as determined by the situation, manifests itself clearly as a mental factor guiding the person's behavior in a new direction, quite independent of the situation in which we perceived him first. At the same time we process the stimulus sequence on the basis of this new *sens;* we no longer see him crossing the street, but, for example, walking back to complete whatever he remembered he had forgotten.

When our perception of the action of another person does not seem to follow from the perceived stimulus situation, then it will mostly mean that the initial *sens* comes into conflict with the subsequent perceived sequence. A perceived conflict between a *sens* and the subsequent sequence may, as we discussed in the previous chapter, result in a number of different consequences. In some instances in particular, when the disagreement is the result of relatively sudden changes in the perceived sequence so that while we perceive a person in the process of carrying out some action we suddenly see him do something different, a new *sens* arises such that we perceive a new intention in the acting person. Accompanying the change in the experienced material sequence, we experience a change of intention in the person.

We can here mention Köhler's contention that any sudden change in what he called "inner direction"—and indeed any sudden event in the subjective life of a person acting naturally—will be expressed as a sudden change in his outward observable activity.[8]

As I mentioned above, when changes take place which do not follow from the stimulus situation in a perceived action sequence, such changes will then often have the result that we perceive a specific change in the inner life of the other person, i.e., that a new intention arises. In my experiments with films, subjects had this experience time and again, when the man in the film does something which does not seem to them to follow from the overt

[8] *Ibid.*, p. 249.

situation. For example, AAH says: "He sat and wrote, suddenly he remembered something," and BG says: "He suddenly remembered the pipe"; in a description, quoted earlier (p. 102), ER says: "then he had to leave, . . . then he thought there was something he had to look up"; and PK perceived the same scene in just about the same way: "He is on his way out and suddenly remembers something which he has to look up." Similar expressions can be found in many experimental reports. When we perceive another person acting in a way which does not appear to us to be determined by the situation in which he finds himself, it may also happen that his intention manifests itself especially clearly to our perception as the factor which determined the sequence. The behavior is no longer determined by the situation; we experience the person as "acting independently" in this actual connection; he is doing something because he "remembers it," because it "occurs to him," because he "likes it," because he "wants to"; in such instances we may clearly perceive the other person as having a free will and it is evident to us that he acts "independently" without being bound by the situation.

When we perceive the action of another person in this way, the psychic aspect of the entity predominates and makes its influence strongly felt. The behavior available to our observation cannot be described here behavioristically without reference to conscious life in the acting person.

But this kind of change in the material sequence does not always result in a perception of the inner life of the acting person. As I said before, we are set to process stimuli on the basis of the given *sens,* and we appear to assume that there is normally some kind of continuity in the mental life of another person. If we perceive him as being in the process of carrying out a particular action, then we are prepared for him to complete it. As described above, a change in the sequence may result in our experiencing a discontinuity in the inner life of the man, but it may also result in our experiencing that the man is influenced by something in the external world and that this is the reason for the change in the behavior sequence. The man's behavior in such cases does not appear to be determined by the situation as it appeared to us, but when the change does take place the behavior becomes the channel whereby a factor in the situation becomes apparent, a factor that influences the action sequence and causes it to change.

In our example of the man who turned back when he was crossing the street we might perceive that someone called to him. The behavior becomes the data through which a factor in the situation manifests itself (a factor which perhaps is evident to us only in this way) and which is perceived as the cause of the change in the behavior sequence.

This condition also occurs in my experiments. PK said, for example: "He turns around suddenly as if someone has touched him on the shoulder, or as if something had happened behind him." And when HT perceives that the man in the film is about to leave, he says: "And when that happened so suddenly, I could imagine that somebody came and called him." LS describes how she perceived the man's behavior at the beginning of the film when he suddenly looks around: "I thought that he got scared about something, that there was a sound which disturbed him, and that it was this he looked for, a dog or a cat or something like that."

We see how the person's behavior is still perceived as determined by the situation; the man does not act independently; the change is not a result of his free will. His behavior appears to be the reaction to an external influence so that we perceive that he notices certain changes in the world around him and that these changes make him behave so that the action that we saw him carrying out is changed or interrupted. Here also the change in the sequence becomes the form under which a change appears in the inner life of the person acting. But here we do not regard the inner change as something "independent," something "he just wants"; here it is apparent to us that the man has seen or heard something (or perhaps has been influenced through another sense) and that this experience has produced the change in his behavior. Along with his behavior,[9] we perceive, perhaps in rather low-rank order, what he perceives. It appears to be true that we generally perceive a person's behavior as co-determined by his actual experience of the environment in which his behavior takes place. As Jørgen Jørgensen says: "We explain the behavior of another person by assuming that it is determined by his experiences." [10]

When we perceive other people, we usually assume that there is a certain continuity in their mental life; and if there is an apparent discontinuity in the action sequence, then the change in the sequence may become the form whereby a change in the surrounding world manifests itself, a change that influences the acting person and is experienced by us as the cause of the discontinuity. If the situation does not permit a change to be perceived in this way, we may sometimes perceive that the man changes intention "on his own," as it were, and for no external reasons; we then experience a discontinuity in his psychic life, implicit in the discontinuity in his behavior.

Not every such change in a perceived action sequence manifests itself to us as a change in the intention of the other person; in order for this to take place, the sequence must be experienced as an action with a *sens* provided by the material sequence. A suffi-

[9] Dr. Iven Reventlow, of the Department of Psychology, has written a description of his observations when he met a person in the street one day suffering from hallucinations. To begin with he thought the man's behavior somewhat strange, but he was not sure what was the matter with him. It is typical of his experience of the hallucinated person that this person's behavior always becomes the form under which entities manifest themselves as they are perceived by the man, entities such as hens and mice and human beings. Reventlow writes for example: "Now I did perceive how hallucinated he really was, because he clearly conducted a conversation with a person who did not exist at all; he looked at the other person, received answers and generally behaved towards the other person in such a way that I get the feeling it is I who cannot see the third person who really is there. It is really this which appears the most interesting that he is so hallucinated and behaves in such a correct manner, that I cannot help but feel that it is really me who is not quite right."

[10] Jørgen Jørgensen, "Remarks Concerning the Concept of Mind and the Problem of Other People's Minds," *Theoria*, 15 (1949), 124–25.

ciently clearly structured situation within which the action takes place must be present to our perception. We must perceive the behavior sequence as having a definite direction, perhaps a certain rhythm, in order for us to perceive that a change takes place in the action sequence at all.

In instances where the behavior of another person is experienced as an entity of low-rank order, where we see that he is "doing something" but do not realize exactly what he is doing, certain parts of the sequence may become the means whereby it becomes evident that "something is going on in him," but we do not perceive what this something is. In order to do so, it is generally necessary that we know something about the current situation and are oriented with regard to a number of conditions concerning it. If we are not oriented, if we have no experience of situations like the current situation, the behavior of the other person will often not appear to us to be a real action. The experience becomes chaotic; if a *sens* arises, it will be vague and imprecise so that great changes may take place in the experienced material sequence without our experiencing any conflict with the low-ranked, vague *sens*. If we perceive only that a person does "something or other," then something very specific must take place in the material sequence in order for a conflict to arise between such a *sens* and the rest of the sequence. The person must, for example, completely stop doing anything, or do something very definite which cannot be regarded as a continuation of the earlier behavior.

Summarizing, we may say that the way in which the action of another person will manifest itself to us depends to a large extent upon how well we know situations of the same, or a similar, kind as the one in which the action sequence is played out; whether we are experienced in the use of the objects that enter into it; and whether we know what "one usually does" in this kind of situation. It is also of great importance whether we know anything about the acting person, or persons of his type; whether we know something about how this kind of man usually behaves. If our orientations

with regard to these factors is weak, the perception of the behavior of others may become very vague and scanty. In such a case
we see that others do something or other, but not what they are
doing, or the experience becomes very disjointed without any connection or transition between the details. There may in such a case
be given a more comprehensive, rather imprecise, *sens;* but normally only very little is given in our experience of the mental life
of the acting person, because in such cases we also have very little
opportunity to perceive such changes in the sequence as could result in the person's inner life standing out clearly for us.

It is possible to illustrate the result when the conditions for
perceiving the behavior of others as actions are not particularly
good by citing a number of protocols from a series of experiments
that I have conducted with patients in the mental hospital at
Ebberødgaard. These experiments were done on individual subjects, one at a time, carried out in the same manner as described
before, and I had a stenographer record the experimenter's questions and the subject's answers.

In general it can be said that these subjects rarely speak spontaneously but mostly respond only in reply to the questions of the
experimenter; their descriptions are generally very brief and only
concerned with the external behavior of the persons in the film,
while they never speak about the inner life of the actors. The subject FP expressed himself about the film as follows:

Experimenter: What did you see in the film?
Subject: First it was the Town Hall, we saw three ladies all the time.
One stood and painted.
E. What happens then?
S. Then there were two other ladies who walked to and fro. One of
them took something down in the bag and the other only walked up.
They changed to another piece.
E. How many were there in the film?
S. Three.
E. And what did the three do?

S. They said good day, and one painted and they went forward and in and greeted each other.

E. What was the end of the story?

S. They packed up, they really packed it all up and left.

E. What did she paint?

S. It was something very strange and tall.

EMH gives the following description:

E. What did you see in the film?

S. I bloody well don't know what it is meant to be.

E. Well, what happened in the film?

S. They stood and painted.

E. What happened next?

S. She stood and painted, I do not know what the other thing means.

E. What did the people in the film do?

S. They stood and talked together.

E. What else?

S. She took some pictures; first she got one, and then she gave one in return to the other lady.

E. Why do you think she did that?

S. How would I know?

E. How many persons were there in the film?

S. Three.

E. What did the others do?

S. One of them walked forwards and backwards all the time.

The protocols show a certain abbreviated experience of the sequence, and some details in the behavior do appear in the experience while the rest remains rather chaotic. This is even more true of KO's description:

E. What did you see in the film?

S. I saw this bag, this bag, they brought here. And then they draw like this, and then they went and then they put it down into the bag and they both of them walked around. Then they left with the bag, they took the bag with them.

E. How many were there?

S. Two. Then they had drawn something like this (she gesticulates). They have drawn something very black. Something like this (makes movements along the table as if writing).

E. How did it end?

S. I saw the lady; they put it on the table.

E. Can you remember more than that?

S. No, it all happened so quickly.

In the case of ELH the description seems to indicate that the sequence was experienced in an even more chaotic and discontinuous manner:

E. What did you see in the film?

S. Two Ladies.

E. What more did you see?

S. (Does not answer).

E. What did the ladies do?

S. There were some magazines—they put them aside.

E. How many persons were there in the film?

S. There were three.

E. And what did they do?

S. They shook hands with each other.

E. And what more did they do?

S. One bowed.

E. And what did the other do?

S. She said good-bye.

E. How did the film begin, what did you see first?

S. A tower.

E. And what did you see then?

S. If we now had had a piano, then we could have played.

It may be that in these experimental subjects certain special conditions which in normal subjects are of little consequence may exercise some influence on the result. The subjects may perhaps have found it difficult to follow what happens in a film, even if it is such a short and relatively simple sequence as the one shown here; and there may be linguistic difficulties when they have to describe what they have seen. But even if such factors may play a role, there is hardly any doubt that the results say something about how persons of low intelligence and little knowledge experience the behavior of others when they encounter situations of which they have little previous knowledge.

3. On Action Potentials

There are a number of factors that play a role in how we will perceive the behavior of other people as an action governed by a *sens* which is evident to us in the material sequence. We have discussed one of these conditions, our degree of knowledge of the situation within which the behavior takes place, and we have touched earlier upon another essential condition, i.e., whether we know anything about the acting person, or about persons of that kind.

If I see a man open a packet of cigarettes and take out a cigarette, there will normally be given the *sens* "he wants to smoke." But if I know the person and know that he is a definite enemy of all tobacco smoking, then I shall not experience that particular behavior sequence as an action with this particular *sens;* I shall not see him about to light a cigarette. In this case "to smoke a cigarette" does not belong to what I shall call the action potentials which I can experience in that person.

Such action potentials may play a great role in the way in which we are set when we perceive other people. It often appears to us that there are certain things a person can and will do while there are others which he cannot or will not do. These action potentials may be given explicitly in and with the perception of others; if, for example, I have an acquaintance of great bodily strength, under certain conditions this may appear for me as a special action potential in the man and influence in a decisive manner how I shall perceive his behavior. If I perceive him as very intelligent, particularly helpful, very wealthy, especially knowledgeable with regard to art, clever in French, and so on, then these things may be given for me as action potentials, which may co-determine how I perceive that the man will act under certain circumstances, and therefore also how I perceive his actions.

We experience both positive and negative action potentials in people, both what a man is able to do and what he is unable to do. If we regard a man as miser, then, to us, he does not have the action potential to give things away with great largesse; if we perceive him as stupid, then he has not, to us, the potential of behaving reasonably; if we perceive him as having no knowledge of Spanish, then he has no possibility of conducting a conversation in that language, and so forth.

Action potentials are perceived traits of the kind which we mentioned at the beginning of Chapter 2. Just as we can perceive how a thing will behave under certain circumstances, to what use it can be put, etc., so we may perceive a person's action potentials so that it is more or less clearly and immediately evident to us what the man may or may not do.

These qualities perceived in others may be provided implicitly in my perception of the other person, and may only stand out clearly when I adopt a set to experience them, or in some other way become directly interested in what the other person may or may not do. Of course, as it is true with most of this kind of entity, my more arbitrary set may make them stand out clearly, but also the situation as I perceive it may be such that certain action potentials in the other person are explicitly evident to my perception.

Action potentials, utility determinations, the "powers" of the things—these are the entities which stand out in perception either because we have rather arbitrarily adopted such a set or because the total perceived situation leads to such an attitude. Rubin called them "easily arising entities" and wanted thereby to draw attention to the fact that these entities are mostly given only implicitly when we perceive people and things, but become explicit and arise in our perception as soon as we take an interest in them.

We should also mention that such easily arising entities play a great role with regard to our whole orientation in daily life. The objects with which we are dealing have a rich reserve, as it were, of traits and characteristics, which are not actively apparent to us at all times, but stand out when we need to perceive them, or when we take a greater interest in them; and thereby is made possible a much more differentiated orientation in a given situation than we should otherwise have. These easily arising qualities in things and persons are like a reserve of knowledge which is not immediately available but is at our disposal when we need to use it.

There are many kinds of such action potentials, and we have some very obvious examples in potentials that are defined by profession and occupation. If we go to church, we may perceive a certain quite definite group of action potentials in the minister; there are a number of things he can do and there are a great number of things he cannot do, while the churchgoers have another group of action potentials. In the hospital we may experience the physician with one group of action potentials, the nurse with another, and the patients with quite a different third group; we may experience in a more or less differentiated and detailed manner what each of them can and cannot do.

If I sit in a bus and think about the action potentials of the conductor, I may experience that there are a number of things which he can do in his position as bus conductor—sell tickets, signal stop and go, direct the passengers—while there are other things which he cannot do: get off at the next stop, sit down and read a newspaper, and many other things which the passengers can do.

These conditions, which I may make clear to myself by thinking about it, are not usually explicitly present in my perception of the bus conductor, but they are present as easily arising entities that stand out as soon as I take an interest in them or when they become of importance for a more considered orientation to the actual situation. In general, as I have said, they are usually implicitly given in my experience of others and they become part of the whole system of attitudes or sets that govern processing when we perceive the behavior of others (see page 81 ff).

If I take an interest in it, it becomes clear that I can perceive such action potentials in all people (and for that matter also in animals). The longer I know the other person and the more knowledge I have regarding him, the more complete and the more differentiated can my perception of his action potentials be: what he can do and what he cannot do.

To gain an overview of all of the many kinds of perceived action potentials with which we may have to deal, I shall divide them into three main areas. There are, however, gradual transitions from one area to another:

(1) What we generally perceive as possible in a person because he belongs to the species *homo sapiens*

(2) What we perceive as typically possible for him because he belongs to a group with which he has certain characteristics in common

(3) What we experience as individually possible for him because of his personal characteristics

The first area comprises the action potentials we perceive in another person if we just experience him as an ordinary member of the human race without any other knowledge of him. It may be evident to us that he has certain action potentials dependent on the structure of the human organism; he may, for example, move, eat, drink, sleep, wake up, handle certain objects, produce sounds. He cannot live under water, break through a wall with his bare hands or—to recall the Bible—he cannot add an inch to his height.[11]

However, it is very rare that we come across a person of whom we only know that he is a human being and nothing else; almost always he will appear to us as belonging to some group or other

[11] Matthew 6:27.

and we may then perceive him with a number of action potentials which belong to the second area. We may perceive him as belonging to a nation and we then include among his action potentials the ability to speak that particular language. We may perceive that he belongs to a particular class in society; that he has a particular religion; belongs to a certain craft, profession, age group; that he is a cannibal, and so on. In all these cases we may perceive that he has a number of action potentials which are typical for that particular group of which we experience him to be a member. When we are dealing with another person, we are set to perceive that he will act as people in his position normally do. As Adam Smith says: "We expect in each rank and profession a degree of those manners which experience has taught us belong to it." [12] In like manner we expect people of different age groups to behave differently: "We expect in old age that gravity and sedateness which its infirmities, its long experience and its worn-out sensibility seem to render both natural and respectable. And we lay our account to find in youth that sensibility, that gaiety and sprightly vivacity which experience teaches us to expect from the lively impressions that all interesting objects are apt to make upon the tender and unpracticed senses of that early period of life." [13]

Among the typical action potentials that we can experience in other people, their attitude toward moral norms, customs and traditions, and ethical standards plays a very important role. Later we shall take a closer look at how decisive these factors are in our whole experience of the behavior of others.

In our daily life a large part of the typical action potentials are such that in a number of situations we have the set and expectation that people will do as we do ourselves—assuming, of course, that under the given circumstances we experience the other people as being of the same kind as ourselves.

Frequently, however, it is evident to us that people can behave

[12] Adam Smith, *The Theory of Moral Sentiments,* 10th ed. (London, 1804), II, 18.
[13] *Ibid.,* p. 19.

differently even if they belong to the same group. We now come to
the third area of action potentials, individual potentials. We may
perceive that it is possible for a man to do one thing or another
because of his special attributes: his constitution, state of health,
intellectual gifts, economic condition, and character.

These individual action potentials cannot be sharply divided
from the typical ones, because it often depends on circumstances
and on our attitude or set whether we shall perceive another person
as representing a type or as a more independent person. The more
we know the other person, the more he will usually appear as an
individual and the less as the representative of a type. If we know
another person really well, a number of his personality traits may
be intrinsic to the experienced stamp, so that his character may
appear to us as a comprehensive behavior pattern (as we have explained in Chapter 2, describing the "experienced stamp"). The
perception of characterological action potentials plays an essential
role for our experience of, and for all our dealings with, other
people to whom we stand in a more intimate relationship. If I experience another person as honest, he has no possibility of behaving
as a traitor, as far as I am concerned. If I experience him as lazy,
as far as I am concerned he cannot undertake energetic and
strenuous work, and so on.

Action potentials are to a large extent exercising an influence on
my set or attitude when I perceive the behavior of another person
and thereby influence what *sens* I shall perceive in a given material
sequence, when this presents itself for me as an action. An example
of how a perceived stamp may, in part, determine the *sens* is given
by the experimental subject LK in her description of the film of
the man who sits and writes. She says, among other things: "He
looked as if he enjoyed acting. The work was not essential. The
most important part was to be seen. He turned around without
any purpose, but I understood later that it was the tobacco he
wanted to get hold of. At first it just appeared as meant to confuse, that is because he is like that." We see how a perceived stamp

creates a set so that the behavior is experienced as without plan and confusing, "without any real *sens*," and that this *sens* first arises during the subsequent sequence. Probably it happens not infrequently when we perceive the behavior of others that the perceived stamp creates a set which has the result that the *sens* of a given behavior becomes blurred or is not experienced at all. Also there are great individual differences with regard to how permanently people perceive these individual action potentials in other persons to be. Some people perceive here a very high degree of certainty and think they know beforehand what others can and cannot do; others are less certain and seem to a greater degree to adopt the set that people may act unexpectedly and that one can never know for certain what they are like.

When we are dealing with other people, they almost always appear in such a way that we perceive (or may perceive) their action potentials. The experiences we have with regard to the individual, with regard to people "of this kind" or with regard to people at large, form the basis of how we shall perceive the behavior of other people. Our different experiences with other people determine which action potentials they appear to have, both in a positive and in a negative direction. For many young children it is probably true that their parents can do everything and know everything, while their experiences in the course of time will in most cases reduce these experienced action potentials to a very large extent.

More generally we can express it in this way: Usually we infer that what a person has been able, or unable, to do in one or more cases he will be able, or unable, to do again. To illustrate this point: Whether the behavior of another person, regarded as achievement, is going to impress us depends among other things on how the action relates to the action potentials with which we experience him as equipped. If the behavior exceeds the perceived possibilities, it will result in our being impressed. For a schoolchild to read is nothing spectacular, but if a four-year-old child can read, it is impressive; that a strong-man lifts 250 pounds is nothing, but if a shrimp of a man lifts such a weight, it impresses us. This phenomenon is often utilized by circus artists who let a particular trick fail time and again so that the spectators (who of course have no clear understanding beforehand of how difficult the achievement is) gradually perceive that this particular trick is so difficult that it lies outside the artist's action potential to execute it. When he finally does carry it out, it impresses the audience much more than it would have otherwise.

Sometimes the action potentials we perceive in others are based on the fact that these persons have attended a course which should make it possible for them to execute certain definite actions. Through piano lessons it is attempted to convey to people the possibility of carrying out the action of playing the piano. Through apprenticeship to a furniture carpenter one wants to provide the person the opportunity of making furniture, and so on. Experience shows, however, that it is not always sufficient to give a certain training and then to assume that the intended possibilities are present. The result may be very different for different people; and one tries with the help of examinations and other tests to assess the result of the training. Very often the examination result is regarded not only as an indication of what a person has learned but as a sign of what he is able to do. And if it then turns out that the examination result is not a valid indication of the person's practical potentials, one is likely to blame the examination—and that is often quite unjustified.

In most cases training must aim at inducing in pupils certain presuppositions which are generally regarded as suitable for the execution of certain forms of action later in life; and the examination is an attempt to measure the extent to which pupils have acquired these presuppositions. Whether the examination result will become a valid expression of the person's practical possibilities does not depend only on how well the examination measures the result of acquisition but also to a large extent on whether the training has served its purpose. In the practical affairs of everyday life we are interested in whether a man is able to execute the actions which belong to his position, when we need him in that role. As the Danish seventeenth-century philosopher and playwright Holberg said: "When I am ill and search for a physician I do not ask for the one who knows Greek and Latin, but for the one who is best able to cure an illness." [14] How far an examination will tell something about a person's possibilities in practice depends just as much on the material to be learned as on the form of the examination itself.

In psychotechnical practice and other branches of applied psychology, attempts are made to measure the prerequisites for achievement apart from those special ones that are the result of teaching or training. Among other things one tries to find a measure of a person's possibilities for acquiring certain information and special skills.[15] It is generally true of psychological tests that one is interested in finding the most reliable index of what the person tested will be able to achieve in daily life. In the field of intelligence testing, for example, one is working with methods which should give a more valid index of the important action determinants of ability and intelligence than daily life experiences are able to give us within a short time.[16]

In our everyday dealings with other people, examination results, intelligence quotients, and other similar test results do not usually play an important role as means whereby a person's action potentials manifest themselves; but under certain circumstances they may be quite important for our perception of that person. And for the specialist they may, in a number of situations, become extremely important in how he will perceive a person. For the psychologist, the physician, the teacher, and others who are generally

[14] Ludvig Holberg, *Epistler*, Tom IV, Epistola 354 (Copenhagen, 1873).

[15] Franz From, "Kundskabsprøver og Evneundersøgelser," *Psykologien og Erhvervslivet*, 1 (1942), 27–32.

[16] Franz From, "Psykologiske prøver—nogle præliminære overvejelser," *Pædagogisk-psykologisk Tidsskrift*, 4 (1944), 153–78.

trained in operating with such measures, the intelligence quotient or the examination result may co-determine their attitude toward the person they are dealing with and exercise a considerable influence on how they experience the other person and his behavior.

4. *When We Do Not Understand Others*

As we have tried to show in the previous section, the way in which we perceive other persons is to a large extent determined by experiences that we have had over the years in our dealings with our fellow man. Not the least our experiences have formed the system of attitudes which we have with regard to how people will act in certain situations; and these attitudes largely determine how our whole perception of social life around us will be formed.

Generally we expect other people to be consistent; we assume that people will do what they usually do in a particular situation. We have the set that habit is a very powerful stabilizing factor in all social behavior, and with William James we regard habit as "the enormous fly-wheel of society," [17] which keeps us all within the bounds of ordinance. But we not only have the set that the individual will do as he usually does, we also expect that he will do as others do. Usually we have the set that people in a given situation will act as others do in the same situation.

It may be as the result of such a set or attitude that a number of my experimental subjects in their description of the film about the artist say that they experienced "the other lady" as an artist (the one who cleanses the brush and fetches a rag to wipe the fingers on). In two group experiments where the subjects produced written descriptions of their experiences, out of the 49 who say anything about her occupation, 24 mention her as "the other artist" (in the film she is not seen as painting). Three of the subjects also experience the third lady in the film, "the guest," as an artist. TH writes: "The third lady herself took out a drawing and gave it to

[17] William James, *Principles of Psychology* (New York, 1918), I, 121.

the woman who painted the Church of Our Lady; this to me seemed to indicate that she also was an artist because they simply exchanged pictures." And GN: "The last arrival appeared also to want to paint. . . . Thereafter she made some further attempts to paint. Finally we see in LHS an example of a *sens* which makes itself felt when the film is finished (see above page 108) because she writes: "Then the artist no. 1 takes her bag from the chair, the last arrival places her bag there instead (I think), and I now thought she was about to paint but then came the end."

That we have the set that people in a given situation will act as they have done before and also that the individual acts as others act when they are in the same situation are two essential factors in the whole system of sets which co-determine the processing of stimuli when we perceive the behavior of others.

When the behavior we perceive in others corresponds to our set, then we "understand" them; i.e., we experience a *sens* in and with the material sequence and this *sens* does not come into conflict with the subsequent sequence as the behavior unfolds. The more knowledge we have regarding a certain person or within a definite behavior area, the more comprehensive is the *sens* we may experience. The actually experienced shorter action sequence may thus become the form under which a longer action sequence manifests itself. If the knowledge is limited, only the more narrow, "actual" situation will manifest itself. Children can often see "what" a person does but not "why." The behavior of adults therefore becomes incomprehensible for them and they ask: "Why does the man do that?" The greater knowledge one has of people, the easier it is to experience the single action as a link in a comprehensive action sequence. If we have special experience within certain areas of social life, it may be possible for us to perceive much wider situations than we otherwise would be able to do. A shrewd politician may perhaps perceive rather immediately a change of government in a distant country as the beginning of a sequence of events which eventually will result in important changes for himself. On the other hand, he may perhaps have to ask his wife what results could be expected to arise from the break between the housemaid and her boy friend. The more experience we have of our fellow man the greater the possibility of experiencing the actual action as the form under which a great number of actions manifest themselves, so that we can calculate, as it were, the future behavior of people ahead of time. (Whether it is the result of a more detailed calculation or whether the perception is more immediate is immaterial.)

Sometimes, however, people behave in a way that does not correspond to our idea of how they have to act. It can happen that peoples' behavior corresponds neither to what they themselves usually do nor to what "is usually done" by everybody else. We have several times touched on the fact that we may encounter forms of behavior where we do not experience any real *sens* as given in and with the material sequence. We do not see what the man intends to do, why he does it, what he is doing—we do not understand the "meaning" of his behavior. As we remarked above (page 71), this will often result in a perception that "there is something wrong" with the other person; he is "odd." How readily this may be evident to us is clearly illustrated in the following description which Tranekjær Rasmussen has provided:

I was riding on my bicycle and a short distance in front of me a man was riding in the same direction as I was. Suddenly I saw him make some movements with his left hand as if he wanted to indicate that he was turning to the left. However, the movements of the hand were not very definite sign-movements; the hand was only put out halfway and immediately afterwards it was pulled back and this was repeated several times. I said to myself: "Is the man going to turn to the left or isn't he?" I can say that I immediately experienced the man as being in a state of "motor aboulia." The more discursive thought processes in myself were not concerned with the "reliability" of this immediate experience but centered entirely on the question, also essential for my own orientation, whether he was going to turn to the left or continue straight forward. The "motor aboulia" or indecisiveness was an experienced quality in the man just about as concretely perceived as the form of his body, etc.

Little by little I had got rather close to him and I now saw something strange in the hand movements. The palm was not extended as one usually does when one is indicating a change of direction before the turn is executed. Only the index finger was extended while the other fingers were bent, as one often does when one is pointing to something. Now suddenly I did not any longer experience the man as being in a state of "motor aboulia" but as a somewhat odd fellow who sat and pointed ahead of himself—also an immediately perceived quality in the man, somewhat of the same kind as the perception one may have of odd people who walk around talking to themselves.

Suddenly he stretched the arm to the fullest extent and pointed, strongly demonstrating, to something high up on a row of houses. I perceived the man to be mad; but only for a moment because immediately afterwards I rode past him and then I saw for the first time that he had a small boy, perhaps his son, in a seat on the bicycle in front of him, and that he was sitting and explaining something while he was pointing at the things he was explaining. What I now saw was also an immediately perceived entity which perhaps could be given the name: "Explaining and showing something to a small boy."

The qualities mentioned which followed upon each other in a sequence were experienced immediately. They were *not* individual stages which I arrived at by discursive deliberations on the line of: this must be an indecisive man, this must be an odd man, this must be a mad man, this must be a man who explains and shows something to a small boy. It was experienced just as immediately as when one experiences a tall man, a short man, a well-dressed man, a shabby man, etc. The experienced qualities mentioned followed upon each other in about the same way as when, for example, visually experienced figures "flip."

When we do not catch the meaning of the behavior of other people, then we do not understand why they behave as they do. And when we do not understand another person, we usually blame the other person. We have mentioned a result of this same tendency above (page 98) where subjects preserved the *sens* which was given for them by perceiving that the man in the film made a mistake. And the same may happen when no *sens* stands out; then we do not realize that we do not possess the premises necessary for finding a meaning in the behavior of the other person but "blame him" and feel that he is odd and behaves unreasonably.

Here we can mention Margaret Mead's description of the Samoans' attitude toward a person who behaves differently from what one would expect. When a Samoan will not do as he, and as "one," usually does—when the child refuses to go to bed, when the mistress refuses her otherwise welcome lover—then this person is said to be "musu," and one normally accepts this without asking about the motives of the other person and does not attempt to make him behave as usual. He is "musu" and there is nothing to be done about it; one does not condemn him and only rarely complains. As these people are immensely dependent on each other and live virtually without any form of privacy, it is obvious that such an attitude with regard to occasional deviating and incomprehensible behavior may provide an essential protection of the individual's personal freedom to act as he wants to in certain situations.[18]

Whether we are concerned with smaller behavior sequences where we are unable to perceive any *sens,* or with action which cannot become a basis for more comprehensive sequences to manifest themselves, the defective understanding of the behavior of other people often has the result that we put a little distance, as it were, between the person acting and ourselves, by experiencing him as "odd." This is obvious with persons who act differently from what we are accustomed to; if they act from premises of which we are ignorant, we do not understand them and find them strange. As the subject EH says (p. 88 above): "He sat and did all those mad things which people who study often do." This attitude may play an important role in our perception of people who belong to another group and who therefore to some extent act on different assumptions from what we ourselves do. It enters into the

[18] Margaret Mead, *Coming of Age in Samoa* (New York, 1950 edition), pp. 86–88.

relationship between parents and children, between men and women, between "town and gown," between employer and employee; it is quite common to regard members of other classes in society as strange. The same holds with regard to the attitude toward other nations and races: the more distant they are from us, the more meaningless and strange do we find their behavior. The more primitive and undeveloped a person is and the fewer hypotheses he has for discovering meaning in the behavior of other people the more he will incline to regard them as "odd."

We tend to regard the forms of our own life pattern as the proper expression of "human nature" and to perceive deviations from our own group's behavior patterns as deviations from normal human behavior. We are centered on our own community and its conditions; we are "community centered," as Sherif says;[19] and we lack perspective when we meet people whose behavior is determined by other premises than those dominant in our own group. That we do not understand the meaning of their behavior is probably a part of the basis for the suspicion, fear, and intolerance toward strangers which we find in nearly all societies. Among the Kiwai Papuans in former times, Landtman tells us in his book about this tribe, any stranger was looked upon more or less as an enemy and his life would be in danger had he fallen into the hands of the people. Hereditary enemies were always killed when encountered and there seems to have been a great temptation to do the same with single individuals or small parties of almost any other tribe except close friends.[20]

This attitude toward strangers is—or was—common among primitive peoples, and it seems to be based on what Ruth Benedict calls one of the oldest human distinctions, the difference in kind between "my own" closed group and the outsider.[21]

All primitive tribes discriminate in this way and place "the others" outside. They are placed outside the law and are without

[19] Muzafer Sherif, *The Psychology of Social Norms* (New York, 1936).
[20] Gunnar Landtman, *The Kiwai Papuans of British New Guinea* (London, 1927), pp. 178–79.
[21] Ruth Benedict, *Patterns of Culture* (New York, 1946), p. 6.

rights, an attitude which has also existed in Europe and has been overcome only slowly and to some extent since the Middle Ages.[22] But the stranger is not only placed "without the law"; he is placed completely outside the human fellowship. A great number of the common names of tribes, such as Zuñi, Déné, and Kiowa, are names by which primitive peoples know themselves and are only their native terms for "the human beings," that is, for themselves. Outside of the closed group there are no human beings.[23] Even if the tribe has much to do with tribes in the neighborhood, they would never even consider regarding "the others" as equals or feel any human relationship with them. Their own group and its way of life are for them the proper human, the only natural and reasonable, way of life; all other ways are experienced as deviant and strange to some degree.

"It would be in vain to assert that the old distinction between a tribesman or a fellow-countryman and a foreigner is dead among ourselves. The prevailing attitude towards war, the readiness with which wars are waged and the notions as to what is allowed in warfare indicates the survival in modern civilization of the ancient feeling that the life, property and general well-being of a foreigner are not on a par with those of a 'compatriot.'" Thus did Westermarck express himself in 1932.[24] The years since then have shown undeniably that the tendency to draw dividing lines between ourselves and "the others" is very much alive and that the inimical attitude toward those who are different has not disappeared in our day and age. Racial prejudice is still strong, even if there are perhaps not many who, as did Sir Samuel Baker, discuss whether the Negroes are of "pre-adamitic" origin, a kind of pseudo-humans who do not spring from our first ancestors.[25]

A characteristic trait in the perception of strangers and their behavior is the not uncommon conviction that the strangers are

[22] Edward Westermarck, *Ethical Relativity* (London, 1932), pp. 197 ff.
[23] Benedict, *Patterns of Culture*, p. 6.
[24] Westermarck, *Ethical Relativity*, p. 199.
[25] S. W. Baker, *The Albert N'yanza Great Basin of the Nile* (London, 1877), pp. 446 ff.

particularly knowledgeable with regard to sorcery. One does not know what they are doing nor what they are able to do; from here it is only a short distance to the attitude that they command mysterious and secret powers. The gypsies are often regarded as sorcerers by the resident population, and in earlier days the same was true of the Lapps in Norway and Sweden. It is typical of primitive tribes that they fear the sorcery of strangers.[26] It is also true in the case of primitive tribes who themselves engage in sorcery that they regard the neighboring tribes as more knowledgeable in sorcery than they themselves are. "It is characteristic," Landtman says, "that all the tribes hold their neighbours to be particularly versed in various kinds of sorcery. The Mawata villagers fear the bushmen and also the Kiwai islanders, and in Kiwai they entertain the same belief regarding the Mawata group in the west and the Wadoba islanders in the east." [27]

When we do not understand the behavior of the strangers, when we perceive that they can do whatever they like, then we see no possibility of predicting how they will and can act in a given situation; they are unpredictable. And the unpredictable we often experience as more or less dangerous, as giving us a feeling of uncertainty. It is decisive for us that we can calculate events ahead of time and take our precautions accordingly; in this way we can, to some extent, secure ourselves against such changes as might in some way constitute a threat. From our knowledge of a sequence of lawful regularities, we can make a prognosis, calculate what will happen under certain circumstances, and act accordingly. The knowledge of a number of natural laws makes possible such predictions over shorter or longer periods; from such elementary questions as determining the interval between sowing the seed and reaping the harvest to complicated predictions of solar eclipses from astronomical observations.

Our surrounding world is constantly changing. We assume that

[26] Margaret Mead, *Sex and Temperament in Three Primitive Societies* (London, 1935), pp. 11–13 and 82.
[27] Landtman, *The Kiwai Papuans of British New Guinea*, p. 326.

the changes are according to laws and through the knowledge of these laws we are in a position to predict what is going to happen. And thereby we acquire the possibility of continually adapting ourselves to such changes as concern our safety. Knowledge of the conditions under which animals and plants exist are necessary presuppositions in order to counteract changes which threaten our need for food; knowledge of illnesses and their causes helps us against threats to our health.

The more we are able to predict changes the greater safety and security we may obtain. In areas where knowledge of regularities is limited, the possibility of making prognoses is small. It is for this reason, for example, that climactic conditions, tornadoes, earthquakes, volcanic eruptions, and floods constitute a threat to the existence of many, a threat against which it is difficult to protect oneself.

A very important part of our surroundings is formed by other human beings and their behavior. Here also we find incessant changes, and changes which may be of extreme importance to our whole existence. Human behavior, however, is a complicated thing. How complicated it is we can comprehend when we compare it with the behavior of animals. Here also we find great variations; but we have discovered some of the laws which govern the behavior of animals in certain situations, even if there is still much to be done. Compared with human behavior the possibilities for variations are strongly limited. We "cannot expect everything" from the animals. A cow cannot give us a poisonous bite, a dog cannot crow as a cockerel in order to deceive us. Man's possibilities for changing his behavior are much more comprehensive. Our behavior is not limited by fixed "instincts," which make actions follow certain patterns with only small variations, as we find in many insects, for example. In any given situation a man often has a quite unimaginable number of alternatives for his behavior.

If human beings chose freely from among all the behavior potentials, then it would be impossible to predict each other's actions, and all cooperation, even human existence, would be extremely difficult. But man is far from utilizing all the potentials for different kinds of behavior which he appears to possess. He places on himself all kinds of limitations to action, analogous to the instincts of animals that determine the behavior sequence in advance. When we have adopted the set that people will act as they themselves usually do and "one" usually does, then there corresponds to this attitude a tendency in people to act exactly in that way. We act to a large extent according to forms which are narrowly determined by tradition and custom.

Habit is the beginning of a rule. "Whatever be the foundation for a certain practice, and however trivial it may be, the unreflecting mind has a tendency to disapprove of any deviation from it for the simple reason that such a deviation is unusual," says Westermarck.[28] Children put great store in the "usual," as do primitives and we ourselves.

This tendency to stay with the usual behavior forms is therefore seen to have an essential importance for social life when we regard it against the background of what we have unraveled about the perception of the behavior of others and about our possibilities for understanding others and for predicting their behavior. When most action forms in a society are fixed, it becomes possible even for the primitive man and for the person with limited experience to predict the behavior of others and to prepare accordingly.

Perhaps this has had a certain importance for the rise and development of ethics, because it may have supplied one base among many others for value judgments with regard to human behavior. That which is in accordance with the rules is good and acceptable because it gives peace of mind, while actions which contradict the laws are bad and undesirable because they are unpredictable and create uncertainty. An ethical attitude proper may have developed from such an attitude among other things.

[28] Edward Westermarck, *The Origin and Development of Moral Ideas* (London 1912), I, 159.

This peace of mind in the daily commerce between men who obey the same rules, i.e., the morals of the society, is stressed by Adam Smith: "Men of virtue only can feel that entire confidence in the conduct and behavior of one another which can, at all times, assure them that they can never either offend or be offended by one another. Vice is always capricious, virtue only is regular and orderly." [29] Virtue is consistent because the virtuous always act according to the commandments of morality; vice is capricious both because actions which do not follow the rules of morality cannot be predicted with the same degree of certainty and because the vicious person sometimes acts according to the commandments and sometimes breaks them. As Frithiof Brandt expresses it: "The bad character often confuses by not always expressing itself." [30]

Rules for behavior also have other functions, as already stated. In many situations they bring relief by freeing us from considering and choosing between different forms of behavior; instead, we simply follow the usual rules. Rules of action may, as it were, abolish a number of goals which we otherwise would have to set for our behavior, observed Tranekjær Rasmussen.[31] But here we shall take a special interest in the fact that the rules of behavior, if they are obeyed, ease our understanding of others. If another person acts according to the rules, then we know what he will do; if he does not follow them, we can expect anything from him. "Nobody knows what he may do."

The less developed a society is (or a group within society) the less background the members have for perceiving comprehensive action situations in each other and thereby for understanding each other's behavior, the more rigorously will it be demanded that rules be kept and obeyed, so that the possibilities of prognosis are upheld. From this point of view it can be regarded as a kind of self-defense when people in traditional societies are intolerant and

[29] *The Theory of Moral Sentiments,* II, 75.
[30] Frithiof Brandt, *Maximer og Sentenser* (Copenhagen, 1945), p. 89, No. 331.
[31] Tranekjær Rasmussen, "Undersøgelser over Erkendelsen" (Manuscript, 1938).

turn with condemnation against all new and unknown ways of behaving; their security is threatened by this, while they feel secure by an adherence to the usual patterns. In children we often meet such a strong attachment to what is usual. They may demand that certain forms of behavior be repeated with absolute exactness. They will have to be put to bed, washed, and so on, according to quite definite rituals which they demand be strictly kept. Perhaps it helps them to obtain an overview of situations which to them appear very involved though they may seem very simple to us. The rules also create stability and the possibility for prediction and adaptation. Most of us follow the rules more faithfully in dealing with people we know less well than we do in the intimate dealings with our nearest relations and friends. We are more formal in a shop, where we are unknown, than we are in the drawing room of the family. Also, within the diplomatic services, where people with very different backgrounds must mix with each other, the rules of etiquette are strictly obeyed, so that, as Adam Smith says, they can be assured that they can never either offend or be offended by one another.

If we encounter situations where we do not know the rules of conduct or where the normally valid rules have been suspended, we feel threatened and lost, as for example when a state of war cancels the ordinary civilian rules for behavior. We cannot predict what the others will do and what will happen at all; this is experienced as a threat and a mental pressure and we work extremely hard to make predictions in spite of the very limited basis which our knowledge of the prevailing conditions offers us for such a prediction.

Let me stress once more that only one aspect of the problem of morality has been looked at here. That morals ease our understanding of the behavior of others is something rather independent of the content of the moral system; what is important here is the system's rigidity and the ease with which it can be understood. If we know the moral system valid in a society, then we can under-

stand the behavior of others, provided they act according to the
rules of that system, irrespective of what the rules prescribe.

5. On Offensive Behavior

We do not agree with Friedrich Paulsen when he maintains
that there exists a definite moral law which in the manner of a
physical law expresses the inner lawfulness of human life. But
he is probably right when he maintains that human life, i.e. a life
with a human, spiritual-historical content, is only possible where
behavior does move within the forms which are expressed in the
formula of the moral law.[32] (By the moral law we then understand the system of moral rules valid in that particular community.)

It is of the greatest importance for all social life that the existing
rules for the behavior in any society are obeyed, by and large; and
it is only one aspect of it that the keeping of the rules may facilitate
our understanding of other people and provide the possibility of
predicting their behavior. Of course, it is not so that all behavior
that does not follow the rules becomes incomprehensible for us, in
the sense that we cannot experience it as an action with a *sens* provided by the material sequence. We do have the more general set
that people normally follow the rules for behavior; but we often
encounter instances where people act without following the rules,
and where nevertheless we experience their behavior as an action,
and where their intention may be evident to us clearly enough.
However, an act of behavior which offends the usual valid rules
will nearly always be experienced in a special way, because the
action acquires a special character for us by being experienced as
an offense against the rules which we experience as valid for the
situation in which the action takes place.

In my investigations of how on the whole we experience the
behavior of other people, I have therefore also taken an interest in

[32] Friedrich Paulsen, *System der Ethik* (Berlin, 1906), I, 16.

a closer study of how we experience the special forms of behavior which consist in breaking the rules for behavior valid in any given group.

Offensive behavior turned out to be particularly suitable for this purpose; and I undertook the following experiment in order to investigate how people in a concrete situation experience an individual who behaves in an offensive manner. During a lecture an undergraduate interrupted the lecturer three times in an increasingly offensive manner and ended by walking out of the auditorium in protest. After an interval of ten minutes the audience was informed that it was part of an experiment prepared beforehand and they were asked to write down a description of what had taken place and to explain what impression it had made on them. The participants were all first-year psychology students, at the end of their first semester; all 49 persons present, with the exception of one, wrote a description. Following the wish of several students the reports were anonymous, with only sex and age stated. In order to make the participants express themselves as freely as possible it was necessary to reveal that it was not a real episode as it otherwise could be feared that many would be rather inhibited in their statements in order not to do harm to a fellow student. Another preponderant reason for not attempting to let the audience believe that it was a real episode was that the request to write the reports would have made many suspect that the episode had been prearranged.

One of the participants, XA, writes the following report:

In the middle of an interesting lecture it happened that a member of the audience suddenly interrupts with a demand to the lecturer to repeat a certain passage in the lecture, "because it appears to me to be somewhat indistinctly explained." At the time I felt a great disdain for the querulous person. My first thought was, I think, "Self-important psychopath" and "stupid ass," but it becomes much worse when a little later he starts on another tirade, which is even more offensive towards the lecturer. Most of the people in the room express their opposition to the interruption and assure the lecturer that they understand the lecture very well. The tense atmosphere which exists around the querulous person culminates when he puts his things together very noisily, closes his bag with a bang and leaves the room with the remark that "this is not for him." I alternate between two theories: (1) that the man has a serious personal conflict with the lecturer and cannot control his emotions; or (2) that the man perhaps is overworked and mentally unbalanced. It did not occur to me for a moment that it was play-acting.

(Only two of the forty-eight reports contain an indication that the experimental subjects suspected the lecturer of having arranged the episode.)

XB describes the episode in the following way:

During the last part of the lecture the teacher is interrupted by a student sitting on one of the benches at the far end of the room. This person asked that an explanation of a drawing on the blackboard be repeated; it was regarding contrast phenomena in the binocular visual field. He then explained that this was the first time he had heard anything about these problems and that he therefore found it difficult to follow. His request for the repetition was made in a very impolite and supercilious tone. The lecturer explained what he had asked for. A little later the same student interrupted again in a still more offensive, impolite and cheeky tone of voice and pointed out that he still did not understand. Now a certain unrest in the auditorium showed that the atmosphere was against the interrupter; it was said from all sides that the explanations were quite sufficiently clear. A moment later he got up, locked his bag in a very demonstrative and noisy manner and left the auditorium saying something like: "I 'regret' that I have to leave but when you cannot explain better I can just as well leave." He was rude and a boor.

All the participants find the person's behavior strange and most of them find it objectionable: 38 of the 48 (about 80 percent) express themselves in a more or less condemnatory manner. Many condemn him out of hand, find his interruption irritating, impolite, stupid and such like; others give him a somewhat wider margin and find his interruption forgivable, understandable or even justified; one subject agrees with him the first time: "I sat just in front of the querulous person, and turned round and said: 'That is right' because I had not understood either what had just been said. Next time he interrupted he sounded very irritated and requested the lecturer to explain himself more clearly—in what I thought to be impolite and unsuitable phrases. This time I did not understand why he interrupted, I thought it sounded offensive," writes XC. Another, XD, sympathizes with his outspoken attitude and likes him for a brief moment, but takes offense because his next interruption sounds aggressive; "his outspokenness bordered on rudeness."

In other instances we find something analogous to what we found in the experiments with the films: when we experience a behavior sequence as an action with a given *sens* so that we see the meaning of the behavior, then the *sens* can take effect both in a forward and in a backward direction with the result that the whole sequence stands out as a totality with one comprehensive *sens*. In this case the whole behavior was experienced as an expression of the same attitude, from the moment when the person opened his mouth the first time until in an offensive manner he banged the door on his departure; his voice, gait, movements, looks, all are made a part of the offensive totality—and some include his past and remember that he has previously acted in a querulous manner.

How does this offensive person appear in the experience of his fellow students? Well, 18 (about 37 percent) experience him just as a type, one of those who "act in such a manner." When he interrupted for the first time, I thought he was of the self-possessed type, who in no way underestimates himself; an unattractive type, but not unknown, writes XE. Frequently, the act of classifying him as a "type" functions at the same time as a pseudo-explanation of the man's behavior, as when for example the person is characterized as a very young man—which the very youngest participant in the experiment does say (XF).

To another 20 (about 42 percent) he appears as an individual with his own stamp, while the remaining 10 (about 21 percent) do not experience him definitely as either a type or as an individual. And those who experience him as an individual nearly all attempt more or less to reach a sort of explanation of the behavior instead of just finding it offensive.

As we have discussed above (page 130), there are great differences with regard to how strongly the psychic aspect stands out in our experience of other people. As long as their behavior follows from the situation and does not show any particular changes, their mental life is mostly given rather vaguely for us, as for example when we experience our fellow students during a lecture. But if the behavior does not follow from the situation, the mental life of the other person may stand out clearly so that we experience it in a more precise and differentiated way; we may, for example, perceive a wish, an act of will, or an intention in the other. But such a perception is insufficient here, where the person's behavior not only does *not* follow from the situation but even offends against the ordinary rules for how one behaves in such a situation; the situation does not become understandable just because one judges that the offender has the intention to act offensively. There are some who perceive the behavior as partly motivated by the man's experience in the actual situation. "The man seemed very bitter, probably mainly because of the laughter his behavior produced," writes XG; and XH: "Now he had become really offended because he had not been heard." It is, however, only a few who perceive the behavior of the man as actually motivated in this manner. A greater number (10) experience something else; they get the immediate impression that the student nurses an old grudge against the lecturer. That means that the person's behavior, otherwise not understandable, is perceived as understandable by becoming the manner in which a more permanent emotional attitude manifests itself—a kind of sentiment in Shand's meaning of the word.

In most cases the experience is not so precisely differentiated; the person appears only as being in an abnormal state which then becomes the explanation of his abnormal behavior. He is nervous, ill, overworked, mentally unbalanced, etc. As XI says: "My first thought was that he must be drunk or in some other way in an abnormal condition. I became very offended because of his behavior which appeared to me irrelevant and stupid." We see that "tout comprendre" is not always "tout pardonner," which the experiment demonstrated most strikingly: there are 23 participants who in one way or another attempt to understand the man's behavior, but 15 of those condemn him in spite of the explanation. And frequently we find "explanations" which must be regarded as camouflaged condemnations when the man is described as stupid, out of his mind, abnormal, very youthful, and other similar expressions. The basis for the condemnation may vary; one member is irritated because he is interrupted in his listening to the lecture. Commonly irritation is expressed over his impoliteness, rudeness, and so on.

Many, however, describe a more complicated attitude. XJ writes, for example:

Everything contracts within one—feeling of shame and dismay—sympathy with the lecturer—need to make amends—look particularly understanding. The comical element in the situation is however evident: one rejoiced a little because one student dared—one would have liked to do it oneself perhaps. But as he walks out in protest, then he overdoes it, the whole room is ready to stand by the lecturer. Now he has gone too far, left the group so far behind that one goes against him, that is too much—one cannot do that. Poor lecturer.

A kind of division takes place in the originally homogenous group, and it ends by the offensive person being ejected. Some of the participants, however, do follow him part of the way; some feel sympathy with him the first time; a single individual directly agrees with him. But when he proceeds, most students dissociate themselves and make sure to get on the right side so that one does not oneself run the risk of ejection; each member agrees with all the others, feels a need to make amends to the lecturer;

one person, XK, notes a "desire to pat the lecturer on the shoulder."

Several go so far as to wish or to expect that the offender would be punished; and while only one person expresses real sympathy with the "sinner," there is general sympathy for the offended lecturer. It looks in some cases as if one is afraid of being suspected of sympathizing with the interrupter [33] and thereby drawing on oneself the anger of the offended authority and the dislike of the majority.

Without entering into this special problem, I shall in this connection briefly remind the reader of Westermarck's theory that society punishes with the utmost severity actions which may arouse the anger of invisible powers in order to prevent the divine wrath from turning against the community itself [34] and also of Émile Durkheim's thesis about the influence which the position of power held by the authority has on the severity of punishment in a society.[35]

A particular aspect of this "taking sides" when the offender is placed outside the group comes to the fore in those subjects who describe how the reactions of the others result in an increase in their own "taking sides," as when XL explains: "The others felt the same as I did; this made me feel even more offended by his behavior." We do have our own conviction about what is suitable, but it is comforting when others think the same. As Adam Smith described it: "Our continual observations upon the conduct of others, insensibly lead us to form to ourselves certain general rules concerning what is fit and proper either to be done or to be avoided. Some of their actions shock all our natural sentiments. We hear everybody about us express the like detestation against them.

---

[33] In a somewhat similar experiment conducted by Captain C. Castenskiold, military psychologist, in a class of young army officers, one of the descriptions finishes as follows: "So far as I am concerned, I felt very ill at ease because of the whole situation, when I got the idea that the captain could possibly think that it was agreed between the interrupter and the rest of the class that he should be provocative."

[34] Westermarck, *The Origin and Development of Moral Ideas,* I, p. 194.

[35] Émile Durkheim, "Deux lois de l'évolution pénale," *L'Année Sociologique,* 4 (1899-1900), 65-95.

This still further confirms and even exasperates our natural sense of their deformity. It satisfies us, that we view them in the proper light, when we see other people view them in the same light." [36]

This experience of common revulsion may tie the individual closer to the group, as it were. "Afterwards a certain relief was felt and a feeling of fellowship with the rest of the audience and with the lecturer. The release was followed by spontaneous laughter," XL says at the end of her description. Others find, however, that the laughter was rather forced. "When the door had closed behind him we all laughed, but I did not really think the experience funny, so the reaction was perhaps a little artificial," writes XM.

Many use the expression that they feel ill at ease; they experience something rather dangerous in the situation without explaining in detail in what the danger consists. In some cases one could perhaps dare to formulate the hypothesis that it is the threatening rupture of the group, reinforced by the contrast to the lecturer's actual authority, which may give rise in the individual to a certain indefinite fear of landing on the wrong side when the group does split. One does not know beforehand with absolute certainty whom the majority will follow.

Perhaps it could hang together with this when so many feel anger, indignation, great dislike, extreme offense, resentment, deep irritation; as XN describes his reaction: "For a moment I sat completely astounded, then felt a strong detestation for the young man and was extremely ill at ease on his behalf." One gets angry with him who breaks the rules; one feels a need again to demonstrate one's own good will and intentions toward the offended person; and one stresses one's own agreement with the group. When the interrupter complained that the lecture was incomprehensible, many shouted that they understood it very well and XK notes: "I was among the first to say aloud that I understood the lecturer's exposition very well."

We see here some of the attitude which Adam Smith describes:

[36] *The Theory of Moral Sentiments,* I, 324–25.

"We resolve never to be guilty of the like, nor ever, upon any account, to render ourselves in this manner the objects of universal disapprobation." [37]

The offense which arises when we perceive conduct which offends the accepted rules for suitable behavior may offer a richly varied and complicated picture which to some extent I think I have succeeded in drawing by the method followed in this essay, a method which it seems to me offers greater possibilities for an unraveling of such problems than do ordinary experimental situations where one attempts to make the subject adopt a neutral attitude.

By this method, where the subjects themselves become involved in the experimental situations and become in a sense co-actors while the action takes place, there is created the possibility for revealing the whole complicated way in which one's own ego and its attitude toward other people become a part of the experience of the behavior of other people. We see certain traits in the immensely complicated, composite emotional patterns which develop, like the intricate patterns formed by ice ferns spreading across a window-pane.

[37] *Ibid.*, p. 325.

Bibliography

ALLPORT, GORDON. *Personality*. London, 1949.

ASCH, S. E. "Forming Impressions of Personality," *Journal of Abnormal and Social Psychology*, 41 (1946).

BAKER, S. W. *The Albert N'yanza Great Basin of the Nile*. London, 1877.

BENEDICT, RUTH. *Patterns of Culture*. New York, 1946.

BLANTON, MARGARET G. "The Behavior of the Human Infant during the First Thirty Days of Life," *Psychological Review*, 24 (1917).

BOGEN, H., and O. LIPMANN (eds.). "Gang und Charakter," *Zeitschrift für angewandte Psychologie*, Beiheft 58 (1931).

BRAGANZ-LEHMANN, MARGA. "Kleid und Persönlichkeit," *Industrielle Psychotechnik* 12 (1935).

BRANDT, FRITHIOF. *Maximer og Sentenser*. Copenhagen, 1945.

———. *Psykologi*. 3rd ed. Copenhagen, 1947.

BRUNER, JEROME S., and CECILE C. GOODMAN. "Value and Needs as Organizing Factors in Perception," *Journal of Abnormal and Social Psychology*, 42 (1947).

BRUNSWICK, EGON, and LOTTE REITER. "Eindruckscharaktere schematisierter Gesichter," *Zeitschrift für Psychologie*, 142 (1938).

CARNAP, RUDOLF. *Der logische Aufbau der Welt*. Berlin, 1928.

CHESTERTON, G. K. *The Father Brown Stories*. London, 1950.

CLEETON, GLEN, and F. B. KNIGHT. "Validity of Character Judgments Based on External Criteria," *Journal of Applied Psychology*, 8 (1924).

DARWIN, CHARLES. *The Descent of Man*. London, 1871, Vols. 1–2.

DURKHEIM, EMILE. "Deux lois de l'évolution pénale," *L'Année Sociologique*, 4 (1899–1900).

ERIKSEN, C. W. "Perceptual Defense as a Function of Unacceptable Needs," *Journal of Abnormal and Social Psychology*, 46 (1951).

FEILBERG, LUDVIG. *Samlede Skrifter*, II, 3rd ed. Copenhagen, 1949.

FELEKY, ANTOINETTE. "The Expression of the Emotions," *Psychological Review*, 21 (1914).

FELEKY, ANTOINETTE. "The Influence of the Emotions on Respiration," *Journal of Experimental Psychology,* 1 (1916).

FISCHER, OTTOKAR. *Das Wunderbuch der Zauberkunst.* Stuttgart, 1929.

FLÜGEL, J. C. *The Psychology of Clothes.* London, 1930.

FREUD, SIGMUND. *Gesammelte Werke,* Bd. 4. London, 1941.

FROM, FRANZ. *Drøm og neurose.* 2nd ed. Copenhagen, 1951.

——. "Kundskabsprøver og Evneundersøgelser," *Psykologien og Erhvervslivet,* 1 (1942).

——. "Psykologiske prøver—nogle præliminære overvejelser," *Pædagogisk-psykologisk Tidsskrift,* 4 (1944).

GARDE, ANNELISE, ALICE SACHS-JACOBSEN, OVE BØJE. *Grafologi i Grundtræk.* Copenhagen, 1946.

HEGEL, G. W. F. *Werke,* Vol. 17. Vollständige Ausg. Berlin, 1835.

HEIDER, F., and M. SIMMEL. "An Experimental Study of Apparent Behavior," *American Journal of Psychology,* 57 (1944).

HERZOG, HERTA. "Stimme und Persönlichkeit," *Zeitschrift für Psychologie,* 130 (1933).

HJELMSLEV, LOUIS. *Omkring sprogteoriens grundlæggelse.* Copenhagen, 1943.

HOFFMANN. *Modern Magic.* London, 1894.

HOLBERG, LUDVIG. *Epistler.* Udg. med oplysende Anmærkninger af Chr. Bruun. Copenhagen, 1873.

JACOBSEN, LIS. *Dansk Sprog. Kritik og Studier.* Copenhagen, 1927.

JAMES, WILLIAM. *Principles of Psychology.* New York, 1918. Vols. 1–2.

JØRGENSEN, JØRGEN. *Psykologi paa biologisk grundlag.* Copenhagen, 1941–46.

——. "Remarks Concerning the Concept of Mind and the Problem of Other People's Minds," *Theoria,* 15 (1949).

KAILA, EINO. *Personlighedens psykologi.* Copenhagen, 1948.

KOFFKA, K. *Principles of Gestalt Psychology.* London, 1936.

KÖHLER, WOLFGANG. *Gestalt Psychology.* New York, 1929.

KRALL, KARL. *Denkende Tiere.* Beiträge zur Tierseelenkunde auf Grund eigener Versuche. Der kluge Hans und meine Pferde Muhammed und Zarif. 3. unveränderte Aufl. Leipzig, 1912.

KRIES, J. VON. "Über die Natur gewisser mit den psychischen Vorgängen verknüpfter Gehirnzustände," *Zeitschrift für Psychologie,* 8 (1895).

LANDTMAN, GUNNAR. *The Kiwai Papuans of British New Guinea.* London, 1927.

LEHMANN, ALFRED. "Om Stemninger i Naturen," *Oversigt over Det Kgl. Danske Videnskabernes Selskabs Forhandlinger,* No. 5 (1913).

LEHTOVAARA, ARVO. "First Impressions," *Studia Psychologica et Paedagogica,* 2 (1948).

LEIBNIZ, G. G. *Opera Omnia.* Tom. 5. Geneva, 1768.

LERSCH, PHILIPP. *Gesicht und Seele.* Munich, 1932.

LOCKE, JOHN. *An Essay Concerning Human Understanding,* 18th ed. Dublin, 1777. Vols. 1–2.

MEAD, MARGARET. *Coming of Age in Samoa.* New York, 1950 edition.

———. *Sex and Temperament in Three Primitive Societies.* London, 1935.

METZGER, WOLFGANG. "Tiefenerscheinungen in optischen Bewegungsfeldern," *Psychologische Forschung,* 20 (1935).

MURRAY, HENRY A. *Explorations in Personality,* New York, 1938.

OERSTED, H. C. *The Soul in Nature.* London, 1852.

PAULSEN, FRIEDRICH. *System der Ethik.* Berlin, 1906. Vols. 1–2.

POSTMAN, LEO, and JEROME BRUNER. "Perception under Stress," *Psychological Review,* 55 (1948).

ROMANES, G. J. *Animal Intelligence.* London, 1904.

RUBIN, EDGAR. "Bemerkungen über unser Wissen von anderen Menschen," *Experimenta Psychologica.* Copenhagen, 1949.

———. "Geräuschverschiebungsversuche," *Acta Psychologica,* 4 (1938) and *Experimenta Psychologica.* Copenhagen, 1949.

SHAND, ALEXANDER. *The Foundations of Character.* London, 1914.

SHERIF, MUZAFER. *The Psychology of Social Norms.* New York, 1936.

SMITH, ADAM. *The Theory of Moral Sentiments,* 10th ed. London, 1804. Vols. 1–2.

STANISLAVSKIJ, K. *En skuespillers arbejde med sig selv (An Actor's Work with Himself).* Copenhagen, 1940.

TEMPLE, WILLIAM. *Works.* London, 1720. Vols. 1–2.

TOLMAN, E. C. "A New Formula for Behaviorism," *Psychological Review,* 29 (1922).

TRANEKJÆR RASMUSSEN, E. Besvarelse af den bundne skriftlige seks Ugers Opgave i Konkurrencen om Professoratet i Filosofi ved Aarhus Universitet, 1938. Manuscript.

———. Undersøgelser over Erkendelsen. 1938. Manuscript.

WATSON, JOHN B. "Psychology as the Behaviorist Views It," *Psychological Review,* 20 (1913).

WATSON, JOHN B., and ROSALIE RAYNER. "Conditioned Emotional Reactions," *Journal of Experimental Psychology,* 3 (1920).

WESTERMARCK, EDWARD. *Ethical Relativity.* London, 1932.

———. *The Origin and Development of Moral Ideas.* London, 1912, Vol. I.

WOLFF, WERNER. "Involuntary Self-Expression in Gait and Other Movements. An Experimental Study," *Character and Personality,* 3 (1934–35).

WUNDT, WILH. *Grundzüge der physiologischen Psychologie,* III, 5th ed. Leipzig, 1903.

Index